TROWBRIDGE · FROME
DEVIZES · MELKSHAM · WARMINSTER

C000225475

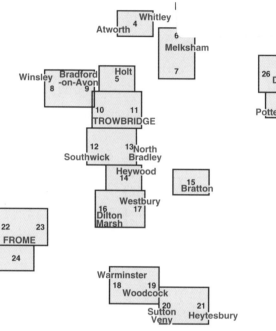

Whitley
Atworth 4
Melksham 6
7
Holt 5
Bradford -on-Avon 9
Winsley 8
10 11
TROWBRIDGE
12 13 North Bradley
Southwick
Heywood 14
Westbury 17
16 Dilton Marsh
22 23
FROME
24
Warminster
18 19
Woodcock
20 21
Sutton Veny Heytesbury
15 Bratton

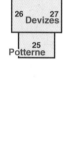

26 27 Devizes
25 Potterne

Scale of street plans: 4 Inches to 1 Mile (unless otherwise stated)

▦ Motorway	
'A' Road / Dual	
'B' Road / Dual	
Minor Road / Dual	
Track	
Pedestrianized	
Railway / Station	
- - - Footpath	

Every effort has been made to verify the accuracy of information in this book but the publishers cannot accept responsibility for expense or loss caused by an error or omission. Information that will be of assistance to the user of the maps will be welcomed.

The representation on these maps of a road, track or path is no evidence of the existence of a right of way.

∿ Stream / River
≋ Canal
→ One-way Street
🅿 Car Park
🄲 Public Convenience
🄸 Tourist Information
✛ Place of Worship
● Post Office

Street plans prepared and published by ESTATE PUBLICATIONS, Bridewell House, TENTERDEN, KENT.
The Publishers acknowledge the co-operation of the local authorities
of towns represented in this atlas.

Ordnance Survey® This product includes mapping data licensed from Ordnance Survey®
with the permission of the Controller of Her Majesty's Stationery Office.

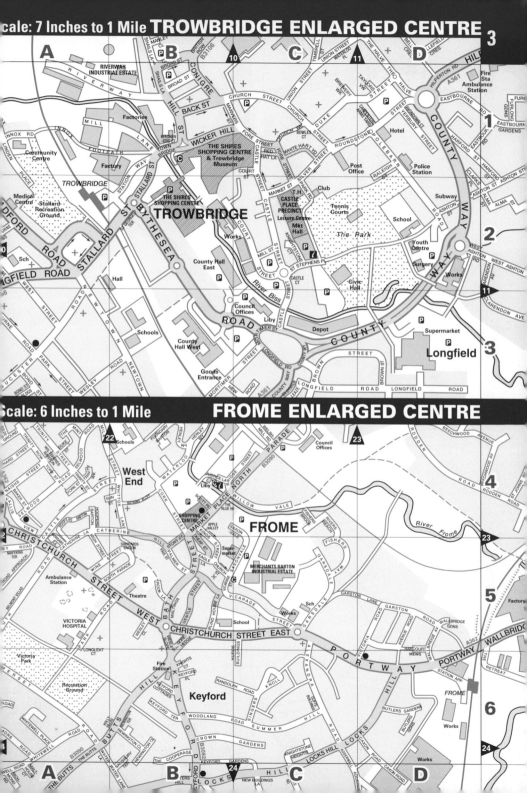

TROWBRIDGE ENLARGED CENTRE

THE SHIRES
SHOPPING CENTRE
& Trowbridge Museum

THE SHIRES
SHOPPING CENTRE

TROWBRIDGE

RIVERWAY
INDUSTRIAL ESTATE

Community
Centre

Medical
Centre

Stallard Recreation
Ground

County Hall
East

Council
Offices

County
Hall West

Goods
Entrance

Longfield

CASTLE
PLACE
PRECINCT
Leisure Centre

Mkt
Hall

Civic
Hall

Depot

Supermarket

The Park

Tennis
Courts

School

Youth
Centre

Surgery

Works

Hotel

Post
Office

Police
Station

Subway

Fire Sta
Ambulance
Station

FROME ENLARGED CENTRE

FROME

West
End

SHOPPING
CENTRE

Schools

Council
Offices

Ambulance
Station

Theatre

VICTORIA
HOSPITAL

Victoria
Park

Recreation
Ground

Keyford

Fire
Station

School

Works

MERCHANTS BARTON
INDUSTRIAL ESTATE

Super-
market

River Frome

Factory

Works

Works

CHRISTCHURCH STREET EAST

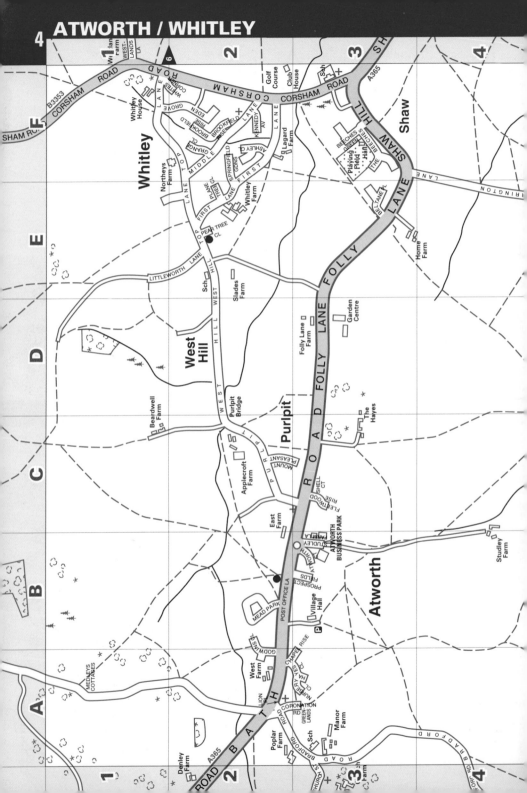

Holt

Staverton

Ham Green

Bradleys Farm

Avon View Farm

River Avon

Hilperton Marsh

The Courts Gardens

Gaston Farm

Manor Farm

Hunts Hall Farm

Woolley Park Farm

Forewoods Common

Great Bradford Wood

Works

Three Lions Mews

Holt Farm

GROUND CORNER

Rec Ground

THE COMMON

THE STREET

HAM GREEN

BRADFORD ROAD

HOLT ROAD

LEIGH ROAD

NEW TERRACE

STAVERTON

B3105

B3107

WOODLAND

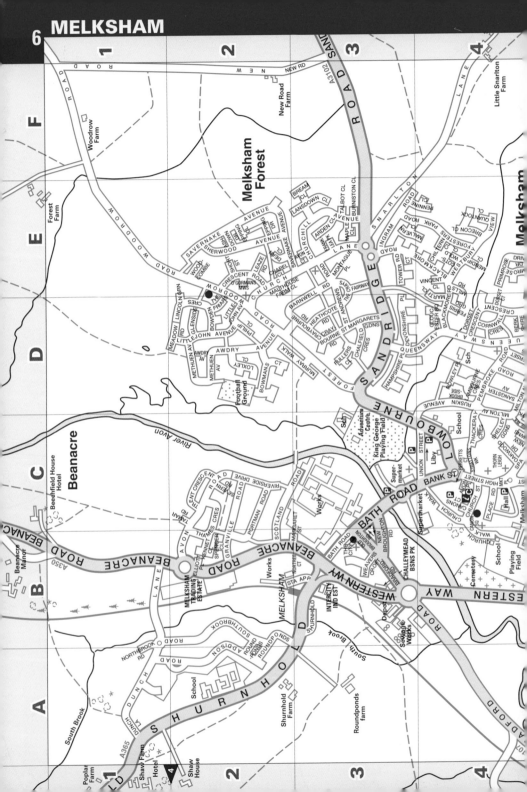

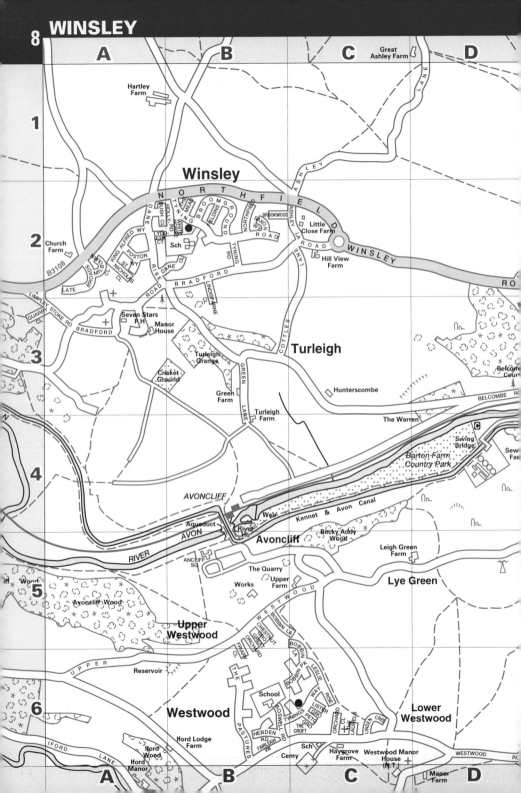

BUSES
TROWBRIDGE - FROME

X34

M-F	M-F	M-F	M-F	M-F
12:55	13:55	15:05	16:25	17:25
12:57	13:57	15:10	16:27	17:27
-	-	-	16:30	-
12:59	13:59	15:12	16:32	17:29
13:03	14:03	15:16	16:36	17:36
13:09	14:09	15:19	16:39	17:38
13:13	14:13	15:21	16:46	17:41
13:19	14:19	15:42	16:57	17:53
13:21	14:21	15:44	16:59	17:55
13:23	14:23	15:46	17:02	17:58
13:28	14:28	15:55	-	18:04
13:30	-	15:57	-	18:06
13:38	14:38	16:03	17:10	18:11
13:42	14:42	16:10	-	18:12
13:49	14:49	16:16	-	18:19
13:52	14:52	16:19	-	18:21
13:58	14:58	16:25	-	R
14:01	15:01	16:31	-	R
14:05	15:05	16:40	-	R

SH	M-F	M-F	M-F
15:14	-	-	17:08
15:18	-	-	17:13
15:20	-	-	17:17
15:25	-	-	17:23
15:27	16:40C	-	17:25
-	-	-	-
-	-	-	-
15:37	16:50	17:14	17:40
-	16:53	17:18	17:45
-	16:55	17:20	17:48
-	16:59	17:25	17:52
-	17:01	17:27	17:54
-	17:04	17:30	17:57
-	-	-	-
-	17:05	17:31	17:57
-	-	-	-
-	17:12	17:38	18:03
-	17:15	17:41	18:06
-	17:16	17:42	18:07
-	R	R	R
-	R	R	R
-	-	-	-
-	R	17:52	R

KEY
M- F Monday to Friday
R = Request stop - set down only
No service on public holidays
Boxed times operate during school holidays only
C = Operates from Trowbridge College,
College Road on college days only
= Operates as 237 service via Holt and Staverton

unt Sch), Newtown, Stallard Street, Conigre, Church Street, Town Hall, Market Street, Castle Street,
Road, A361, Semington, A350, MELKSHAM, Semington Road, King Street, Market Place (Lowbourne,
rnhold, George Ward Sch) High Street, Bank Street, Bath Road, (Forward - New Broughton Road;
, Melksham Road, Bath Road, Rowden Hill, Bath Road, (to college - The Bridge,
ber Street to Chippenham Bus Stn

RTHER DETAILS

	M-F	SH	M-F	M-F	M-F	M-F	M-F
			237				
CHIPPENHAM, Bus Stn - Bay 2	6:55	7:57	7:20	.	8:55	9:55	10:55
Chippenham Bridge	6:56	7:58	-	.	8:57	9:57	10:57
Chippenham College - depart	.	-	.	.	-	-	-
Chippenham Hospital	6:58	8:02	-	.	8:59	9:59	10:59
Notton, Whitehall Garden centre	7:02	8:06	7:25	.	9:03	10:03	11:03
Lacock	7:04	8:09	-	.	9:09	10:09	11:09
Beanacre, The Peacock	7:05	8:13	-	.	9:13	10:13	11:13
MELKSHAM, Market Place	7:12	8:17	7:37	.	9:19	10:19	11:19
Berryfields	7:14	8:19	#	.	9:21	10:21	11:21
Semington, Somerset Arms	7:16	8:21	#	.	9:23	10:23	11:23
Hilperton, Church Street	7:20	8:26	#	.	9:28	10:28	11:28
Horse Road	7:24	8:28	#	.	9:30	10:30	11:30
TROWBRIDGE, Town Hall, Arrive	7:30	8:36	8:18	.	9:38	10:38	11:38
TROWBRIDGE, Town Hall, Depart	-	-	8:18	.	9:42	10:42	11:42
Frome Rd, College Road	-	-	8:22	8:49	9:49	10:49	11:49
Southwick, Church	-	-	.	8:52	9:52	10:52	11:52
Beckington, Bus Shelter	-	-	.	8:56	9:58	10:58	11:58
Oldford, The Ship	-	-	.	9:01	10:01	11:01	12:01
FROME, Market Place	-	-	.	9:05	10:05	11:05	12:05

	M-F	M-F	M-F	M-F	M-F	M-F	M-F
FROME, Market Place	7:00	-	9:33	10:33	11:33	12:33	13:33
Oldford, The Ship	7:03	-	9:36	10:36	11:36	12:36	13:38
Beckington, Bus Shelter	7:06	-	9:40	10:40	11:40	12:40	13:40
Southwick, Church	7:12	-	9:46	10:46	11:46	12:46	13:46
Frome Rd, Whiterow Park	7:14	-	9:48	10:48	11:48	12:48	13:48
St Augustines School	.	-	-	-	-	-	-
John O Gaunt School	.	-	-	-	-	-	-
TROWBRIDGE, Town Hall, Depart	7:20	9:00	10:00	11:00	12:00	13:00	14:00
Hilperton Marsh, Horse Road	-	9:06	10:06	11:06	12:06	13:06	14:06
Hilperton, Church Street	.	9:09	10:09	11:09	12:09	13:09	14:09
Semington, Somerset Arms	7:30	9:13	10:13	11:13	12:13	13:13	14:13
Berryfields	7:32	9:15	10:15	11:15	12:15	13:15	14:15
MELKSHAM, Market Place, arr	7:35	9:18	10:18	11:18	12:18	13:18	14:18
Melksham, Halifax Road	7:43	-	-	-	-	-	-
MELKSHAM Market Place, dep	7:53	9:23	10:25	11:25	12:25	13:25	14:25
George Ward School	8:00	.	-	-	-	-	-
Beanacre, The Peacock	8:08	9:30	10:32	11:32	12:32	13:32	14:32
Lacock, George Inn	8:11	9:33	10:35	11:35	12:35	13:35	14:35
Notton, White Garden centre	8:14	9:34	10:37	11:37	12:37	13:37	14:37
Chippenham Hospital	8:18	9:38	10:41	11:41	12:41	13:41	14:41
Chippenham Town Bridge	8:20	R	R	R	R	R	R
Chippenham College	8:30	-	-	-	-	-	-
CHIPPENHAM, Bus Stn - Bay 2	8:35	9:47	10:49	11:49	12:49	13:49	14:49

Route Description

FROME, Market Place, North Parade, Fromefield, Bath Road, Oldford Hill, Beckington, Rode, TROWBRIDGE, Frome Road, (John Fore Street, Wicker Hill, Shails Hill, British Row, Islington, The Down, Wyke Road, Horse Road, Hill Street, Church Street, Trowb Forest Road, Church Lane, Blackmore Road, Queensway, Spa Road, Halifax Road, Bader Park, Falcon Way, A365, Western Wa Return - Old Broughton Road), Bradford Road, Western Way, Beanacre Road, Beanacre, (Lacock), Notton, Patterdown, CHIPPE Station Hill, Cocklebury Road, Sadlers Mead, Cocklebury Road, Station Hill, The Bridge) Avenue La Fleche, Gladstone Road Ro

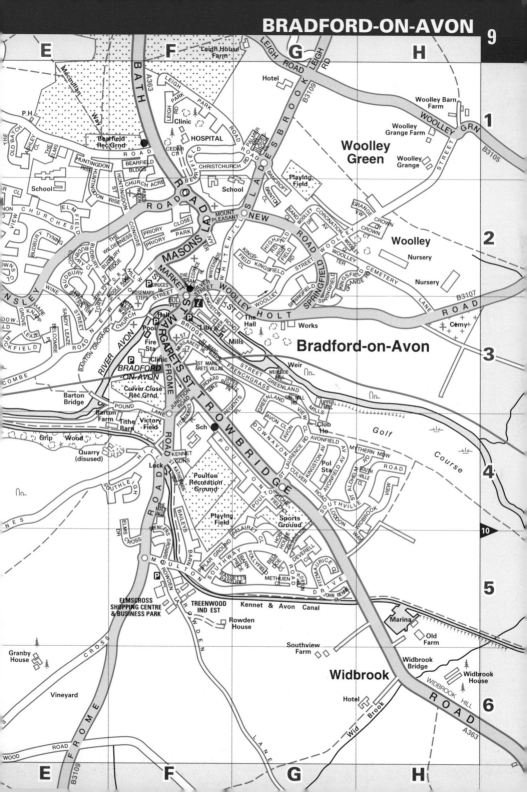

E   F   A   G   H

B3105

LANE WHADDON LANE

1

2

3

4

5

6

Hilperton Marsh Farm

ROAD HILL

STREET

HAMMOND WAY

MARSH

ROAD

NEW TERRACE

GREENHILL CLOSE

NEWLEAZE

Hilperton Marsh

Sch

Hall

Playing Field

THE KNAP

CHURCH ST

Hilperton

St Michaels CL

CHERRY GDNS

Nursery CL

WOODMILL TER

COPPER BEECHES

DEVIZES ROAD

DEVIZES RD

DEVIZES

WELL LANE

STOURTON

NORRIS RD

BIRCH GDNS

FIELDS WELL

CRESSWELL DR

HILPERTON RD

Cemetery

VICTORIA ROAD

ALBERT ROAD

OSBORNE

DOWNSIDE PK

DOWNSIDE PK

FULNEY CL

MIDDLE LANE

TROWBRIDGE RD

STOKELE

ASHTON RISE

AFSLEY CL

LACOCK GDNS

LACOCK DRIVE

HILPERTON DR

A361

Palmers Copse

PARK

WOODHOUSE GDNS

NEWHURST

ROAD

ASHTON

School

WINDERMERE RD

THE CONISTON RD

THE MOUNT

RULFORD RD

CLEVELAND GDNS

GRASMERE

SPRING GDNS

RODWELL PK

RODWELL PK

RAGLEY GRO

PAGLEH GRO

Hotel

ROAD

HILPERTON

VICTORIA RD

KENTON DR

ALBANY CLOSE

THE BEECHES

HALFWAY CL

PEPPERACRE LA

RAVENSCROFT

HALFWAY LA

DRIVE

School

CASTLEY RD

FAVERO LA

PAINTERS

GIBBS

MEAD

HACKETT

PLACE

Nursery

Comm Centre

Super-market

LEAZE

MEAD

CHANCE

WY

LYNESLEY

CHASE

PROBY PL

PAVELY GDNS

WALNES LEY

Paxcroft Brook

Brook Farm

MOYLE

MOYLE PK

MOYLE PARK

ORCH WY

Paxcroft Mead

HILPERTON

COUNTY WY

Fire Station Amb Sta

FURLONG GDNS

EASTBOURNE STREET

BARN GLEBE

LARK SPUR

YARROW DOWN

THE PADDOCKS

MAPLECROFT

Sch

TROWBRIDGE

ST THOMAS

BELLEFIELD CRES

STANCOMB AV

QUARTERWAY LA

EASTBOURNE RD

EAST

Pol Sta

Sch

WEST ASHTON RD

CLARENDON AVENUE

ALMA ST

LWR ALM ST

HEATHER SHAW

PAXCROFT

SMITHY

WELL CL

KENWOOD WY

HONEYMANS CL

SLOWGROVE CL

PAXCROFT WY

GADBY RD

LYNEHAM WAY

SOUTH

CLARENCE RD

HWOOD RD

AMOUR ACRE

GREEN

ROAD

BEATRICE WY

CLARENDON ROAD

LODGE CT

Trowbridge Rugby Club

PARSONAGE RD

PARSON CL

STOKEHILL

COBRA SH RISE

CORNBR SH RISE

GATE

MOYLE

CASTEL CL

CASTEL

GREEN LANE

ROAD ASHTON

Green Lane Farm

Longfield

Supermarket

WEST ASHTON RD

JASMINE

MAGNOLIA RISE

WOODLANDS EDGE

CHEVIOT CL

BROAD CLOTH CL

ALUM CL

QUILLING CL

LAVENDER

EAST

WEST

BROADCLOTH LA

Blackball Bridge

SOUTHWAY

Arnolds Hill

A A366 London Bridge **B** WINGFIELD 10 Sports Centre **C** ool **D**

WINGFIELD ROAD RICHMOND RD DANING ROAD KEW DR Playing Fields ROAD GLOUCES PARK WESLEY RD

1 **Studley Green** HUNGERFORD ELM ELMDALE ROAD HENDERSON WATERWORKS GLADSTONE STREET ST Trowbridge Town Football Ground HARM PL

WESTFIELD GLEBE ROSEVIEW ROAD EASTVIEW ROAD ELMDALE RD PITMAN AVENUE ROCK ROAD ALLEN RD LANSDOWN ROAD ASKE YEOMAN COUNTY W ALASTAIR RUTLAND CRESC

A366 DRIVE WESTFIELD CL TALBOT ROAD HIGH RD BLAIR RD PITMAN AV PITMAN BRADLEY WY ARMS ROW ASHME

KENSINGTON CHASE WATER ROAD BECK School SHAFTES MANOR CL Schools MARBLE GRO YEOMAN ROAD RUTLAND CRES

2 SHERIDON DR SUMMERLEAZE MANORBURY CT Sports Centre Playing Fields ST JOHNS HOSPITAL CARLTON THE CRE

KINGSW REGENTS SUMMERLEAZE MANOR CL WARBURTON CL CEDAR GRO GROVE HOLBOR

LAMBROK CL ALDERBURY FIELD WAY FRAMPTON ROAD Wiltshire College GROVE LARCH GRO WALNUT GRO Sports Ground BAYDON WILTSHIRE

LAMBROK ST JOHNS CRES WEBBERS LOANS BOROUGH RISE ST ARETS Trowbridge Garden Centre Theatre BEECH ALMOND GRO HAZEL SYCAMORE GRO HAWTHORN GRO STREET W. Will D.C. Off

ROAD ACORN MDW WHITEROW PARK WHITEROW PARK COLLEGE RD COLLEGE WILLOW GROVE LILAC GRO CREST GRO Sch GROVE LANE SILVER

WHITEROW CRES CHURCH FIELDS FROME SILVER MDWS SANDRINGHAM ALDER GRO Hall HEDDINGTON

Upper Studley CHURCH LANE THE HASTINGS WHITE ROW HILL FIRS HILL SILVER STREET THE POPLARS SPRING MEADOWS WINDSOR DR HOLYROOD RD BALMORAL RD WINTERSLOW KINGSDOWN BEW LANGLEY BROUGHTON ROAD

3 *Southwick Country Park* White Row Bridge ROAD BALMORAL KINGSTON CL MARSTON Sch

P Southwick Court Farm BOUNDARY WALK BOUNDARY WK Sports Field

4 Moat AXE AND CLEAVER L Bramble Farm

ST ANNES FLEUR DE LYS GARDENS Park Farm

5 FAIRFIELD MDWS Arnold Road Corner TESSIDE WYNSOME CHANTRY SNEAP BROOKMEAD CLEAVER THE RANK PINE WK OAK BIRCHEN ASH

A3610 FROME HOLLIS WAY CHANTRY STREET **Southwick** AXE AND WINCHESTER CL OAK DR OAK ASH AZE

HOGGIN Sch CHANTRY GDNS BRIDGE BREACH LANE ORCHARD DRIVE

WESLEY ORCHARD STHFIELD HOLLIS BLIND WYNSOME Berryfield Farm Organ Pool Farm ROAD SOUTHWICK CHURCH

ME ROAD LAMBERTS MARSH WESLEY STREET BRADLEY Home Farm GRAYS

6 Blue Barn Farm Greenhill Farm STREET LANE

Mutton Farm Poles Hole Farm SOME STREET 14

A **B** **C** **D**

Longfield

ORCHARD RD
OCHADEN
BRINLEY
CHERRY
LONGFIELD ROAD
SOUTHWAY
WEAVERS
SHEEPCOTE
BROADCLOTH
SPINNERS
GARDENS FMN
WORSTEAD
QUILLING WAY
MARGREAVES
FLEECE
COTTS
HEWITT
RYELAND
WAY
HANKER
SHEARMAN

11
CAEVIOL
CL
BROAD
CLOTH LA
ALUM
SHOT
EAST
LAVENDER
CL
BROADCLOTH LA
MAGNO
RISE
WEST
WOODLANDS

Blackball
Bridge
WOODLANDS
EDGE

Blackball
Hatch

**Lower
Studley**

River Biss

PEMBROKE
CL
WILTON
BURNET
WHITE
HORSE
VIEW
RD
SHREWTON
CHERITON
PL
CLOCK
CL
CAMPION DR
COMFREY
SPRELL
CL
LEIGH
CL
LEIGH

Biss
Farm

ASHTON ROAD WEST

Drynham

DRYNHAM
PARK
ROAD
DRYNHAM
LANE

Drynham Park
Farm

2

*Biss
Wood*

SPITFIRE
RAIL PARK

DRYNHAM
DROVE
DRYNHAM
LA
DRYNHAM
LANE

AINTREE

**WHITE HORSE
BUSINESS PARK**

AVENUE
EPSOM
ASCOT
SANDOWN
CENTRE
GOODWOOD
CL
EASOM
EPSOM
RD
AINTREE

Lower Biss
Farm

3

ASHTON
ROAD

B3097
YARNBROOK ROAD
BRATTON RD
ORCHARD

4

**North
Bradley**

WINDSOR RD
NEWMARKET

Little Common
Farm

**WHITE HORSE
BUSINESS PARK**

Ashton Hill
Farm

Yarsbrook
Farm

WOODSIDE
COTTAGES

P

LITTLE
COMMON
WOODMARSH
WESTBURY
ROAD

Kings
Farm

Manor
Farm

W E S T B U R Y

Homefield
Farm

MATTLA

*Flowers
Wood*

KETTLE
LANE

5

RWICK
COLLEGE

Rec
Ground

LANE

ROAD
WEST

Yarnbrook

ASHTON

6

HAWKERIDGE

Woodlands
Farm

ROAD
WEST
A350

Kettle Lane
Farm

B3097
ROAD
HAWKERIDGE

14

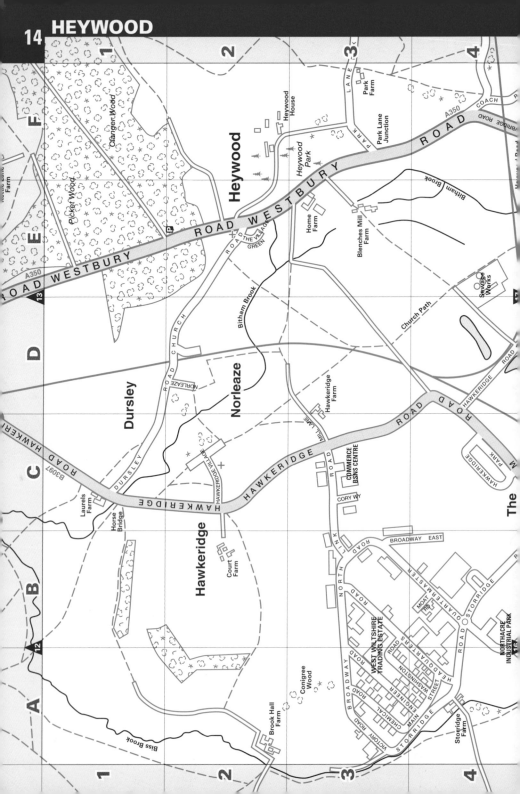

Heywood

Heywood House

Park Farm

Park Lane Junction

Heywood Park

COACH ROAD

/BRIDGE ROAD

A350

ROAD

Bitham Brook

WESTBURY ROAD

Home Farm

THE VILLAGE GREEN

Blenches Mill Farm

Sewage Works

Church Path

ROAD WESTBURY

A350

13

Dursley

Norleaze

CHURCH ROAD

NORLEAZE

Hawkeridge Farm

Bitham Brook

HAWKERIDGE ROAD

ROAD

Road

HAWKERIDGE ROAD

The

B3097 HAWKERIDGE ROAD

HAWKERIDGE

Dursley

HAWKERIDGE VILLAGE

MILL LANE

COMMERCE BSNS CENTRE

CORY WY

HAWKERIDGE PARK

Laurels Farm

Horse Bridge

Hawkeridge

Court Farm

NORTH LINK ROAD

ROAD

BROADWAY EAST

WEST WILTSHIRE TRADING ESTATE

CHEMICAL ROAD

ENGINEER ROAD

WASHINGTON

HEADQUARTERS ROAD

STORRIDGE ROAD

QUARTERMASTER ROAD

LYON

NORTHACRE INDUSTRIAL PARK

Biss Brook

Conigree Wood

Brook Hall Farm

BROADWAY ROAD

VICTORY ROAD

MAIN STREET

Storridge Farm

Picket Wood

Clanger Wood

Horse Lane Farm

Sunnycroft Farm
Court
COWLEAZE
BAZELEAZE
WAY BAYNTON
BAYNTON
LANE
SOUR LITTLE LANE
BERRY RD
COURT
Slades Farm
CHARLTON HILL
SALISBURY HOLLOW
Tinhead Hill
LONG HOLLOW
LONG HOLLOW
Westdown Farm

B3098
WESTER
ROAD

LONG HOLLOW
LONG
HOLLOW
LONG HOLLOW

THE WEIR
GREENSIDE CT
RIVERSIDE
BANNER PL
THE WEIR
ROAD
TINHEAD
COURN LANE
TINHEAD ROAD
THE CITY

Patcombe Hill

Edington Hill

NASTERY
ROAD
Works
Fish Pond
Works

MONASTERY RD
MONASTERY RD
PARSON AGE LA
DOWNSVIEW
GREATWOODS
MANOR CT
GREATER
LONGLANDS
LANE

Mound
Mound
Mound
Mound
Tumuli
Picquet Hill
Luccombe Bottom

IN MEAD
LOWER
ROAD
GREATER
Edington

Sandy Lane

IMBER ROAD
IMBER
ROAD

Hudds Mill Farm
Wood Bridge
LOWER ROAD

Fitzroy Farm

Bratton

Crossroads Farm
ROAD
LANE CAPPS

ASHTON COOMBE
KINGS MEAD
PEAR TREE ORCH
GILBERTS MEAD
CLOVER CL
CHAPEL CL
REDLANDS
CROSSING
Sch
EMMS
CARPEN-TERS LA
MANOR FIELDS
STRADBROOK
THE BALL
TYNING LA
SOUTHAY
ETHENDUN
THE PICQUET
HOLME LA
UPPER GARSTON
THE BUTTS
GARSTON LA
COMBE LANE

MELBOURNE ST
LOWER ROAD
WEST

IMBER
ROAD
CHURCH

Combe Bottom

TROWBRIDGE
ROAD
Bridge Farm

COURT
LANE
LOWER ROAD
COURT ORCHARD
ROSENHEIM RISE
TBURY RD
LOWER WESTBURY ROAD
RY ROAD
B3098
WESTBURY ROAD
CASTLE ROAD
PORT WAY
COMBE LA

1 2 3 4
A B C D E F

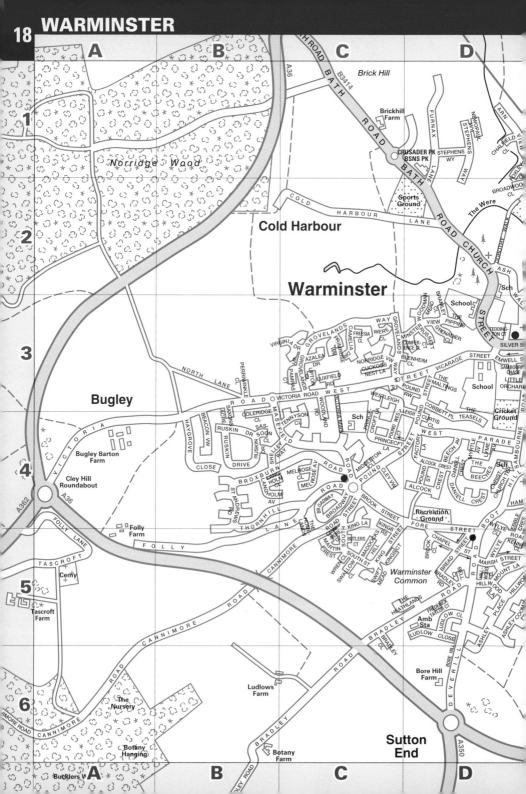

A   B   C   D

1

Norridge Wood

Brick Hill

Brickhill Farm

CRUSADER PK BSNS PK

2

Cold Harbour

COLD HARBOUR LANE

Sports Ground

The Were

Warminster

School

3

Bugley

NORTH LANE

Grovelands

PERIWINKLE CT

Sch

School

Cricket Ground

Teasels

4

Bugley Barton Farm

Cley Hill Roundabout

VICTORIA ROAD WEST

HAYGROVE

BEACON VW

RUSKIN DR

RUSKIN DRIVE

CLOSE

BROXBURN

SHELLEY WAY

TENNYSON CL

Sch

MELROSE

MELROSE AV

POUND

CLEY VW

The Beeches

Sch

5

Folly Farm

ST ANDREWS RD

THORNHILL LANE

FOLLY

CANNIMORE ROAD

Broadway

Brook Street

Recreation Ground

Warminster Common

Amb Sta

TASCROFT

Cemy

Tascroft Farm

6

The Nursery

CANNIMORE ROAD

Ludlows Farm

BRADLEY ROAD

DEVERILL ROAD

Bore Hill Farm

Botany Hanging

Botany Farm

Sutton End

Bucklers W

A   B   C   D

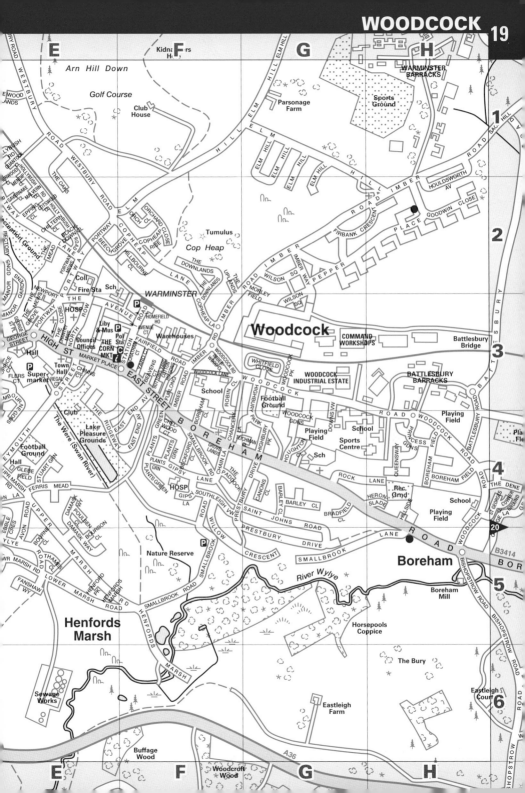

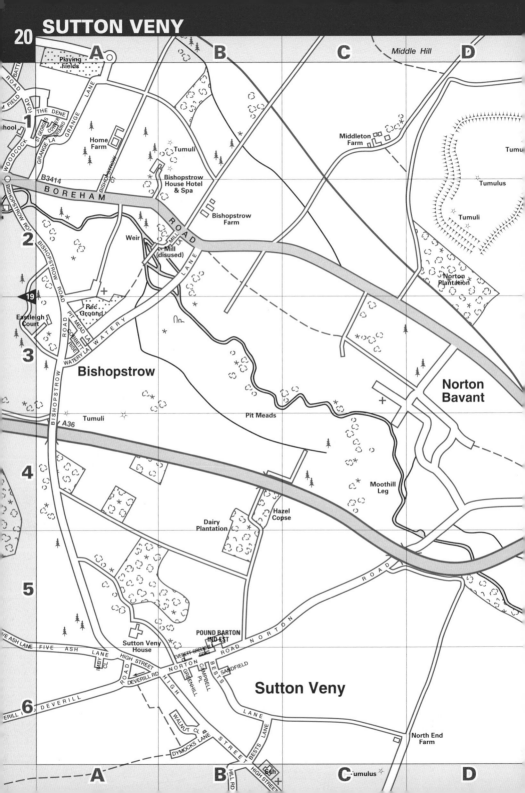

Middle Hill

Playing fields

THE DENE

Home Farm

Tumuli

School

B3414

BOREHAM ROAD

Bishopstrow House Hotel & Spa

Bishopstrow Farm

Middleton Farm

Tumuli

Tumulus

Tumulus

Tumuli

Weir

Mill (disused)

MILL LANE

Norton Plantation

Eastleigh Court

Rec Ground

PIT MEAD ROAD

WATERY LA

WATERY

Bishopstrow

Norton Bavant

Tumuli

A36

Pit Meads

BISHOPSTROW ROAD

Moothill Leg

Hazel Copse

Dairy Plantation

NORTON

ROAD

Pound Barton Ind Est

Sutton Veny House

Everett Green Clo

Greenhill

Campbell Pl

Sandfield

FIVE ASH LANE

HIGH STREET

NORTON ROAD

BESTS

Sutton Veny

WALNUT CL

DYMOCKS LANE

DEVERILL RD

HIGH

STREET

HILL RD

BESTS LANE

LANE

North End Farm

Cumulus

WOODCOCK

BISHOPSTROW RO

BISHOPSTROW ROAD

GRANGE LA

GRANGE LANE

BISHOPSTROW CT

DEVERILL

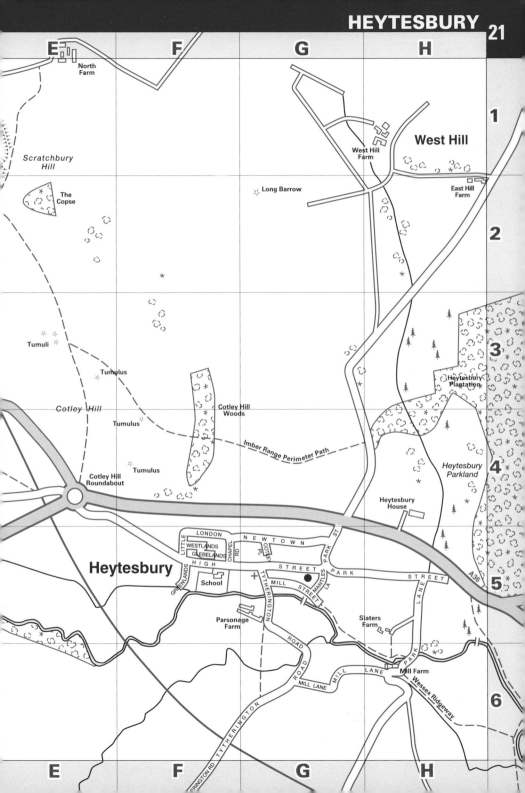

A36

A361

Rodden

BY-PASS

Feltham Bridge

Feltham Farm

Bleet's Farm

Marsh Farm

EAST WOODLANDS RD

FROME

Adderwell

Southfield Farm

The Mount

FELTHAM LANE

BIRCHILL

BLATCHBRIDGE

B3092

Blatchbridge

River Frome

Claybatch Farm

Brick Chimney's Farm

Little Keyford

LITTLE KEYFORD LANE

Sandy's Hill Farm

BULLS QUARRY RD

MARSTON PARK IND EST

B3090

MARSTON RD

A361 MARSTON RD

Tytherington

Marston Gate

MARSTON ROAD

Supermarket

Super-store

Lower Keyford

Keyford Farm

SANDY'S HILL LANE

MARSTON TRADING ESTATE

HANDLEMAKER ROAD

MARSTON

COURTS BARTON

MASONS

The Butts

Critchill

Whitemill Farm

Gibbet Hill

CRITCHILL

WHITEMILL LANE

THE BUTTS ROAD

ROSSITERS ROAD

CULVERHILL

THE MOUNT

Keyford

B3092

FROME 23

Works

LOCKS

ADDERWELL

WALKER RD

CHARLES RD

NEW FOSTER BUILDINGS

FOSTER RD

STONEWALL TCE

AUSTIN CLOSE

FELTHAM DR

SOUTHFIELDS

THE MOUNTS

HILLSIDE

SUNNY SIDE

SUNNYSIDE

LONG GROUND

TOWER VW

Sch

BUTTS HILL

THE BUTTS

WEYMOUTH HILL

RETREAT

Parklands Farm

SLEIGHT LANE

Sleight Farm

SLEIGHT COTTAGES

Potterne Wood

Crookwood Farm

F

GREEN LANE HOSPITAL

GREEN LANE

Grubbes Wood

E

STROUD LANE

BYRON ROAD

WYATT ROAD

ELLIOTT ROAD

THOMAS WYATT ROAD

HAM RD

CHAPEL

BURN RD

THURM RD

BOWES CT

WYATT CT

COOT CT

THOWL

Sch

BYRON

CLOCK TOWER LODGE

DREWS POND LA

Stroud Hill Farm

STROUD LANE

D

Nine Hills

Drews Pond

Montecello Farm

Potterne Field

Potterne

C

THE FAIRWAY

BROAD

ROAD

26

Rangebourne Mill

THE POTTERNE

Sandfield Farm

FIRS HILL WY

ST MARYS CL

ST MARYS CL

SILVER ST

SILVER STREET

Cemy

BROWNLEAZE LA

BLACKBERRY LA

HIGHLANDS

BLACK BERRY LA

BLACKBERRY LA

TOLLBAR CL

RYELEAZE

HIGHLANDS

THE BUTTS

Sch

COXHILL LANE

BLOUNTS CT

BLOUNTS CT

BLOUNTS CT

BLOUNTS CT

B

Furzehill Farm

MILL RD

ST

DUCK ST

HIGH

COXHILL

A360

A

FURZE HILL LANE

WHISTLEY ROAD

ROAD

COURT HILL

COURT HILL

T HILL COURT

A   B   C   D

1

CONSCIENCES

CONSCIENCES LANE

CONSCIENCES LANE

Tanis

TANIS

Rowde Field Farm

Iron Peartree Farm

Roundway Park

Tanis Farm

2

A342

ST DEVIZES ROAD

VIZES RD   ST DEVIZES ROAD

Consciences Bridge

Lower Farm

DEVIZES

Camping & Caravan Site

Deer Park

Newlands Wood

Belvedere Wood

Cemetery

3

Dunkirk

ROAD

DUNKIRK HILL

Devizes

DYEHOUSE LANE

Browfort Kennet D.C. Offices

HIGH LAWN

ROAD

WAIBLINGEN WAY

BELLEVUE RD

WAIBLINGEN WAY

AVON TER

RISTON CL

GEN WY

SHEPPARD CL

ROTHERSTONE

ROTHERSTONE

HOSP

Sch

THE NURSERY

NORTHGATE STREET

WHARF

WHARF

Brewery

Pol Sta

COUCH LANE

SNUFF LA

COMMERCIAL

4

Flight of Locks

MAYENNE PLACE

MAYENNE PLACE

BATH RD BSNS CENTRE

Rec. Ground

DUNDAS

CAEN HILL GDNS

Kennet & Avon Canal

Locks

Prison Bridge

Locks

Park VW

BEAN CLERC ST

AVON RD

AVON ROAD

SALISBURY ST

ROAD

BEAN CLERC

BATH   ROAD

Locks

St Josephs Sch

Sch

MOYNE CLOSE

GELCOMBE CL

THE SIDINGS

STATION RD

STATION

NORTH GATE

GAS LANE

WEST LEY

BRIDGE

NEW PARK STREET

NEW MKT.

MKT PL

LEWIS CT

THE MKT

CASTLE RD

CASTLE LA

CASTLE

CASTLE

PC

P

P

i

LITTLE BRITOX

HIGH ST

ST JOHNS ST

MARYPT

RENDE

ROAD   BATH

A361

ROAD BATH

Avon RD

AVON ROAD

Sewage Works

DEVIZES CASTLE

CASTLE ST JOHNS

CHURCH WK

HILL

CHARLES ST

THE PARK

Mus

ST JOHNS ST LONG

5

Park Pale

Gilletts Farm

WEST VIEW CRESCENT

WEST VIEW CRES

HILLWORTH

THE MOORLANDS

WREN CL

ESTCOURT

HILLWORTH ROAD

HILLWORTH GDNS

HILLWORTH

Hillworth Park

CORNWALL CRESCENT

HARTMOOR CL

QUEENS ROAD

BROADLEAS

ROAD

SOUTHGATE

6

Old Park

Old Park Farm

HILL VIEW

HARTFIELD

HARTMOOR

Broadleas Gardens

Pine Walk

BROADLEAS

BROADLEAS

BROADLEAS ROAD

BROADLEAS CRESCENT

POTTERNE

A360

WICK LA

ORCHARD

POND LA

THE FAIRWAY

WOODLAND WY

WOODLAND

A   B   25   C   D

The Index includes some names for which there is insufficient space on the maps. These names are indicated by an * and are followed by the nearest adjoining thoroughfare.

Churchill Av SN12 6 E3
hurchill Rd BA11 22 B6
hurchlands BA14 13 E6
hurchward Dr BA11 23 F3
larence BA14 11 F6
larendon Av BA14 11 E6
larendon Rd BA14 11 E6
lare St BA14 3 D1
lay Cl BA13 11 E4
leveland Gdns BA14 11 E4
leveland Way BA13 17 E4
ley Vw BA12 18 C4
lifts Bldgs BA11 3 C6
link Farm Ct BA11 23 F4
link Rd BA11 23 F4
lipsham Rise BA14 10 B5
livey BA13 11 F6
lock Tower Lodge SN10 25 D1
loford Cl BA14 10 B5
lothier Leaze BA14 3 C3
loven Ct SN12 7 D5
lover Grass BA13 15 B3
lumber Dr BA11 22 C4
lydesdale Cl BA14 12 D2
loch Rd BA13 14 F4
oal La BA11 22 A2
oalash La BA11 22 A2
oalway La BA11 23 G3
oate La SN10 27 G2
obbett Pl BA12 18 D3
obbett Rise BA12 20 A3
ock Hill BA14 10 B4
ock Hill House Ct BA14 10 B5
old Harbour La BA12 18 C2
oleridge Cl BA12 18 B4
ollege Gdns BA14 13 E5
ollege Rd BA14 12 B2
ollett Way BA11 23 G3
ollingbourne Cl BA14 13 E3
olston Rd SN10 26 C3
ombe La BA11 15 B4
omfrey Cl BA14 13 E2
ommand Workshops BA12 19 G3
ommerce Bsns Centre BA13 14 C3
ommercial Rd SN10 26 D3
ompton Dr BA14 11 E1
ompton Gdns BA11 23 G3
onference BA12 18 D3
onigre BA13 3 B1
onigre Cl SN12 7 C5
onigre Rd BA14 9 F2
oniston Rd BA14 11 E4
onsciences La SN10 26 A1
onway Cres SN12 7 C6
ooke Ct SN10 25 D1
opheap La BA12 19 F2
opheap Rise BA12 19 F2
oping St SN10 27 E5
opper Beeches BA14 11 G3
oppice Cl BA12 19 E3
oppice Hill BA15 9 F2
orbin Rd BA14 11 G5
orfe Rd SN12 7 C5
ork St BA11 3 B4
ornbrash Rise BA14 11 G5
orner Ground BA12 20 A1
ornfield Rd SN10 27 F4
ornflower Way SN12 7 D5
ornwall Cres, Devizes SN10 26 D5
ornwall Cres, Melksham SN12 6 D4
oronation Av BA15 9 G2
oronation Rd, Atworth SN12 4 A2
oronation Rd, Frome BA11 23 E5
oronation Rd, Melksham SN12 7 D5
oronation St BA14 13 E1
orsham Rd BA14 4 F1
ory Way BA13 14 C3
otley Pl BA12 21 G5
otswold Cl, Melksham SN12 6 E4
otswold Cl, Warminster BA12 19 E2
ottles La BA15 8 B3
otton House Gdns BA12 18 F3
ouch La SN10 26 D4
ounty Way BA14 3 D1
ourt Hill SN10 25 A4
ourt La, Bratton BA13 15 A3
ourt La, Edington BA13 15 F1
ourt Orchard BA14 15 A4
ourt St BA14 3 C2
ourts Barton BA11 24 B2
owleaze La BA14 15 E1
owslip Cl SN10 27 G3
owslip Mws SN12 7 D5
oxhill La SN10 25 A4
randon Lea BA14 5 E1
ranesbill Rd SN10 27 F3
ranmore Cl BA14 10 B5
ranmore Ct BA14 24 B2
ranmore Vw BA11 24 B2
rawley Cres BA14 10 B6
raybourne Rd SN12 6 D3
rescent Rd BA14 3 D1
resswell Dr BA14 11 H3

Critch Hill BA11 22 A6
Critchill Ct BA11 24 B1
Critchill Ct BA11 22 A6
Critchill Gro BA11 24 B1
Critchill Rd BA11 22 A6
Cromwell Rd SN10 27 F5
Croscombe Gdns BA11 23 G4
Cross St BA14 10 D5
Crown Ct BA15 5 D2
Crown Gdns BA11 3 B6
Crusader Pk Bsns Pk BA12 18 C1
Cuckoo Hill BA11 22 C3
Cuckoo La BA11 22 B2
Cuckoos Nest La BA12 18 C3
Culver Rd BA15 9 G4
Culverhill BA11 24 D1
Cunnington Cl SN10 27 F4
Curtis Cl BA12 18 D4
Cusance Way BA14 11 G5
Cygnet Cl SN10 27 G2
Cypress Way BA11 23 F3

Daisy Cl SN12 7 D5
Dales Rd BA13 17 E4
Damask Way BA14 19 E4
Dane Cl BA15 8 A2
Dane Rise BA15 8 A2
Daniell Crest BA12 18 D4
Danvers Way BA14 17 H2
Dark La BA11 23 H2
Davies Dr SN10 27 H1
De Havilland Pl SN12 7 H8
Dean Cl, Frome BA11 23 G4
Dean Cl, Melksham SN12 6 E2
Delamere Rd BA14 11 E4
Delmore Rd BA11 3 A6
Delta Cl BA11 22 C5
Delta St BA11 22 C5
Dene Cl BA13 17 F5
Deverell Cl BA15 9 G5
Deverill Rd, Sutton Veny BA12 20 A6
Deverill Rd, Warminster BA12 18 D6
Devizes Gdn Ind Est SN10 27 F2
Devizes Rd, Devizes SN10 26 A2
Devizes Rd, Melksham SN12 7 E6
Devizes Rd, Trowbridge BA14 11 G3
Devon Dr BA13 17 G1
Devonshire Pl SN12 6 D3
Dog Kennel La BA13 17 F5
Dommetts La BA11 23 H2
Dorcan Ct BA13 17 F5
Dorothy Walk BA13 18 D2
Dorset Cl BA11 22 B5
Dorset Cres SN12 6 D4
Dorset Cl SN12 6 D4
Dorset Dr BA13 17 G1
Doulting Ct BA11 23 G3
Dovecote Cl BA14 10 B6
Dowding Ct SN12 7 D7
Dowding Way SN12 7 D7
Downavon BA15 9 G4
Downhayes Rd BA14 10 D4
Downlands Rd SN10 27 E6
Downs Cl BA15 9 E2
Downs Vw, Bradford-on-Avon BA15 8 D2
Downs Vw, Warminster BA12 19 G4
Downside Pk BA14 11 E3
Downside Vw BA14 11 E4
Downsview BA13 15 D2
Downsview Rd BA13 17 F2
Drakes Av SN10 27 E5
Drews Pond La SN10 26 D6
Druces Walk BA15 9 F2
Drynham Dro BA14 13 E4
Drynham La BA14 13 E3
Drynham Pk BA14 13 E1
Drynham Rd BA14 13 E1
Duck St SN10 25 A4
Duke St, Frome BA11 3 A4
Duke St, Trowbridge BA14 3 C1
Dunch La SN12 6 A1
Dunford Cl BA14 26 A4
Dunford Ct BA14 13 E1
Dunkirk Hill SN10 26 B3
Dursley Rd, Trowbridge BA14 12 D1
Dursley Rd, Westbury BA13 14 C1
Dutts BA13 16 B5
Duxford Cl SN12 7 D8
Dyehouse La SN10 26 D3
Dyers Close La SN10 22 C5
Dymocks La BA12 20 B6
Dymott Sq BA14 11 G2

Eagle La BA11 3 B5
East End Av BA12 19 F4
East St BA12 19 F3
East Woodlands Rd BA11 24 B5
Eastbourne Gdns BA14 11 E5
Eastbourne Rd BA14 11 E5
Easthill BA11 23 F6

Eastleigh Cl, Devizes SN10 27 F5
Eastleigh Cl, Frome BA11 22 D3
Eastleigh Rd SN10 27 F5
Eastview Rd BA14 12 B1
Eastwood Cl BA11 22 A6
Ebbie Cres BA12 18 D4
Ecos Cl BA11 22 B6
Eden Gro SN10 4 F2
Eden Vale Rd BA13 17 F3
Edward Rd SN10 27 E5
Edward St BA13 17 G2
Egford Hill BA11 22 A4
Egford La BA11 22 A5
Elcombe Cl BA14 12 D3
Elcombe Gdns SN10 26 C4
Elizabeth Cl SN12 7 A7
Elizabeth Dr SN10 27 F4
Elliot Pl BA14 10 A5
Elliott Cl BA11 22 D4
Elliott Cl SN10 25 D1
Elliott Pl SN12 6 B2
Elm Cl, Melksham SN12 7 D6
Elm Cl, North Bradley BA14 12 D5
Elm Cl, Staverton BA14 5 C1
Elm Ct SN10 27 E7
Elm Gro BA13 17 E3
Elm Hill BA12 19 F2
Elm Leigh BA11 23 F4
Elm Tree Cl SN10 27 F5
Elm Tree Gdns SN10 27 G5
Elmdale Cl BA14 12 B1
Elmdale Rd BA14 12 B1
Elmfield BA15 9 E2
Elms Cross BA15 9 F6
Elms Cross Dr BA15 9 F6
Elmscross Bsns Pk BA15 9 F5
Elmscross Shopping Centre BA15 9 F5
Emms La BA13 15 B3
Emwell St BA12 18 D3
Engineer Rd BA13 14 A4
Epping Cl, Melksham SN12 6 E2
Epping Cl, Warminster BA12 19 E2
Epping Dr SN12 6 E2
Epsom Rd BA14 13 F4
Epsom Rd BA14 13 F4
Epsom Sq BA14 13 F4
Estcourt Cres SN10 27 E4
Estcourt Hill SN10 26 D5
Estcourt St SN10 27 E4
Ethendun BA13 15 B4
Everett Cl BA12 20 B6
Everleigh Cl BA14 13 E3

Factory La BA14 18 D4
Fairdown Av BA13 17 H3
Fairfield Cl BA11 22 D3
Fairfield Mdws BA14 12 A5
Fairfield Rd BA12 19 F3
Fairhaven BA13 16 D5
Fairleigh Vw BA15 9 F5
Fairway SN12 6 E3
Fairways BA13 16 D5
Fairwood Cl BA14 11 G4
Fairwood Rd BA13 16 D5
Fairwood Trading Est BA13 16 C5
Falcon Way SN12 7 E7
Fanshaw Way BA12 19 E5
Farleigh Av, Melksham SN12 7 C5
Farleigh Av, Trowbridge BA14 10 A6
Farleigh Cl BA13 17 F1
Farley Cl BA11 23 F4
Farm Cl BA14 10 B4
Farmhouse Dr BA11 22 C3
Farrant Rd BA11 22 B5
Faverolle Way BA14 11 G4
Fell Rd BA13 17 E3
Feltham Dr BA11 24 D1
Feltham La BA11 24 D2
Ferguson Rd SN10 27 F6
Fermoy BA11 23 F4
Ferozeshah Rd SN10 27 H1
Ferris Gro SN12 6 D3
Ferris Mead BA12 19 E4
Field Cl BA13 17 G1
Field Way BA14 12 B2
Fieldins BA15 8 B2
Firbank Cres BA14 19 G2
Firs Hill La BA11 23 G1
First La SN12 4 E2
Firwood Rd BA11 3 A6
Fishers Brook BA11 3 C4
Fishers Way BA11 3 C4
Fitzmaurice Cl BA15 9 G5
Fitzmaurice Pl BA15 9 F4
Five Ash La BA12 20 A6
Fleece Cotts BA14 3 E1
Fleetwood Rise BA14 4 C3
Fleur De Lys Dr BA14 12 B4
Flints Cl BA11 3 D1
Folly La, Melksham SN12 4 D3

Folly La, Warminster BA12 18 A4/5
Folly Rd SN10 27 F1
Follyfield BA15 9 G5
Fordson Rd SN10 27 F6
Fore St, Trowbridge BA14 3 C1
Fore St, Warminster BA12 18 D4
Fore St, Westbury BA13 17 G2
Forest Rd, Frome BA11 23 E3
Forest Rd, Melksham SN12 6 D3
Foresters Park Rd SN12 6 E4
Forty Acres Rd SN10 27 F4
Foster Rd BA11 24 D1
Foundary Barton BA11 3 B4
Fountain Ct BA13 17 G2
Foxbury Cl BA11 22 D4
Foxglove Cl SN10 7 E5
Foxglove Dr BA14 11 E2
Foxley Cl BA12 18 D2
Frampton Ct BA14 13 F2
Francis St BA14 10 C4
Frankleda Ms SN12 6 E3
Frederick Taylor Ct BA13 18 D5
Freesia Cl BA14 18 C3
Frenchgrass BA15 9 F3
Friars Cl BA13 16 C5
Friary Cl BA15 8 B5
Frogmore Rd BA13 17 F1
Frome Rd, Bradford-on-Avon BA15 9 A6
Frome Rd, Frome BA11 23 F1
Frome Rd, Southwick BA14 12 B2
Frome Rd, Trowbridge BA14 12 A5
Fromefield BA11 22 D5
Fulford Rd BA14 11 F4
Fullers Cl BA14 6 D3
Fulmar Cl SN12 7 E7
Fulney Cl BA14 11 F3
Furlong BA11 19 F3
Furlong Gdns BA14 11 E5
Furnax La BA12 18 D1
Furze Hill La SN10 25 A1

Gables Cl SN10 27 F6
Gabriel Cl BA13 23 G3
Gains La SN10 27 G4
Gainsborough Rise BA14 12 B2
Garsdale BA11 3 C5
Garston La BA11 3 C5
Garston Rd BA11 3 D5
Gaston BA13 5 D2
Gentle St BA11 3 B5
George St, Trowbridge BA14 10 D5
George St, Warminster BA12 19 E3
George Street Pl BA12 19 E3
Georges Grnd BA11 24 C2
Georgian Ct BA11 24 B1
Gibbs Cl BA13 17 G2
Gibbs Leaze BA14 11 G4
Gibson Cl SN12 7 E7
Gilberts Mead BA13 15 B3
Gipsy La, Frome BA11 23 E2
Gipsy La, Trowbridge BA14 5 E1
Gipsy La, Warminster BA12 19 F4
Gladstone Rd BA14 12 C1
Glebe Fld BA12 19 E4
Glebe Rd BA13 12 B1
Glebelands BA12 21 F5
Glenside SN12 6 D2
Gloucester Rd BA14 3 A3
Gloucester Sq SN12 6 D4
Gloucester Walk BA13 17 G1
Godwins Cl SN12 4 A2
Gooch Cl BA11 23 G4
Goodwin Cl BA12 19 H2
Goodwood Cl BA14 13 F4
Gooselands BA13 17 E4
Gorehedge BA11 3 B5
Goulds Grnd BA11 3 A4
Goulds La BA11 3 A4
Granary Cl SN10 27 F4
Granary Rd SN10 27 F4
Grange Cl SN12 4 F2
Grange Cl SN12 20 A1
Grange Rd BA11 22 D3
Grange Vw BA15 9 G2
Granville Rd SN10 6 B2
Granville Ter BA14 13 E1
Grasmere, Melksham SN12 7 E7
Grasmere, Trowbridge BA14 11 F4
Grays Leaze BA14 12 D6
Great Orchard BA15 8 B5
Great Pks BA14 5 F1
Great Roc Rd BA13 17 E2
Great Western Cl SN10 26 D4
Greater La BA13 15 D2
Greatwoods BA13 15 D2
Green Cl, Bradford-on-Avon BA15 8 B3
Green La, Devizes SN10 27 E6

Green La, Frome BA11 22 B6
Green La, Trowbridge BA14 11 F6
Green La, Westbury BA13 17 F4
Green Lane Cl BA11 22 B6
Green Ter BA14 10 D4
Greenacres BA13 16 A6
Greenfield Rd SN10 27 E6
Greenhill BA12 20 B6
Greenhill Gdns, Trowbridge BA14 11 G2
Greenhill Gdns, Warminster BA12 21 F5
Greenhills BA13 15 E2
Greenland Mills BA15 9 G3
Greenland Way BA15 9 G3
Greenlands, Melksham SN12 4 A3
Greenlands, Warminster BA12 21 F5
Greenway Gdns BA14 11 F3
Greenwood Rd SN12 7 B5
Grenadier Cl BA13 18 D3
Ground Cnr BA14 5 D2
Grove Ct BA14 12 D2
Grove La BA11 24 C1
Grove Leaze BA15 9 E3
Grove Mead BA11 24 B2
Grovelands BA12 19 F4
Grovelands Way BA12 12 D3
Gryphon Cl BA13 17 E2
Gundry Cl SN10 27 F4

Hackett Pl BA14 11 G4
Hackney Way BA13 17 E3
Haden Rd BA14 13 E1
Halfway Cl BA14 11 F4
Halfway La BA14 11 F5
Halifax Rd SN12 7 D7
Ham Cl BA14 5 D2
Ham Grn BA14 5 D2
Ham Rd BA13 17 E1
Hambleton Av SN10 27 G1
Hammond Way BA14 11 G1
Hampshire Gdns BA13 17 G1
Hampshire Pl BA13 6 D3
Hampton Cl BA14 7 E7
Hampton La BA12 18 D4
Hampton Mws BA13 17 G4
Handlemaker Rd BA11 24 B2
Hanewell Rise BA14 11 H3
Hanover Cl BA14 11 E1
Hanover Gdns BA14 24 B1
Harcourt Bsns Pk BA14 11 E2
Harcourt Mws BA11 3 D6
Hardie Walk SN12 6 C4
Hare & Hounds St SN10 27 E4
Hare Knapp BA15 9 E3
Harebell Way SN10 27 G3
Harford St BA14 3 D1
Hargreaves Rd BA14 13 F1
Harmony Pl BA14 12 D1
Harrier Ct SN12 7 D6
Hartfield SN10 26 C6
Hartmoor Cl SN10 26 C5
Hartmoor Rd SN10 26 C6
Harvard Cl SN12 7 F7
Havelock St BA14 12 D1
Hawcroft BA14 5 E1
Hawkeridge Pk BA13 14 C4
Hawkeridge Rd, Trowbridge BA14 13 F6
Hawkeridge Rd, Westbury BA13 14 C2
Hawkeridge Village BA13 14 C2
Hawksworth Cl BA11 23 G3
Hawthorn Gro, Trowbridge BA14 12 D2
Hawthorn Gro, Westbury BA13 17 E3
Hawthorn Rd BA13 17 E3
Hayes Cl, Melksham SN12 4 A3
Hayes Cl, Trowbridge BA14 11 E2
Haygrove Cl BA12 18 B4
Haynes Rd BA13 17 G3
Hayward Pl BA13 17 F1
Hazel Gro, Trowbridge BA14 12 C3
Hazel Gro, Westbury BA13 17 E3
Hazelwood Rd BA13 7 B5
Headquarters Rd BA13 14 A4
Heath Dr BA11 22 D4
Heathcote Rd SN12 6 D3
Heather Av SN12 6 D3
Heather Cl BA13 17 F2
Heather Shaw BA14 11 E5
Hebden Rd BA15 8 B6
Heddington Cl BA14 10 A3
Helmdon Rd BA14 10 A5
Helps Well Rd BA14 11 H3
Henderson Cl BA14 12 C1
Henford Pk BA12 19 E5
Henfords Marsh BA12 19 E5
Henley Way BA15 7 D8
Hercules Way SN12 7 D8
Herons Cl SN12 7 E7
Heronslade BA12 19 H4
Hewitt Cl BA14 13 F1
High Lawn SN10 26 B4

High St, Devizes SN10 26 D4
High St,
  Dilton Marsh BA13 16 A6
High St, Frome BA11 3 A5
High St,
  Heytesbury BA12 21 F5
High St, Melksham SN12 6 C4
High St, Potterne SN10 25 A4
High St,
  Sutton Veny BA12 20 A6
High St,
  Warminster BA12 19 E3
High St, Westbury BA13 17 G3
Highbury Pk BA12 19 G3
Highfield Rd BA15 9 G2
Highlands SN10 25 B3
Hill Grnd BA11 22 C5
Hill St, Hilperton BA14 11 F1
Hill St, Trowbridge BA14 11 H3
Hill Vw SN10 26 C6
Hillbourne Cl BA12 19 F2
Hillside BA12 19 H4
Hillside Av BA11 24 D2
Hillside Pk BA13 17 H3
Hillwood Cl BA12 18 D5
Hillwood La BA12 18 D5
Hillworth Gdns SN10 26 D5
Hillworth Rd SN10 26 C5
Hilperton Dr BA14 11 G4
Hilperton Rd BA14 11 E5
Hobhouse Cl BA15 9 G5
Hodders Cl BA11 22 C5
Hodge Cl SN10 27 F4
Holbrook La BA14 12 D2
Holbrook Vale SN12 7 A7
Hollis Way BA14 12 A5
Holly Ct BA11 23 F3
Holly Villas BA11 3 A6
Hollybush Cl BA15 8 B2
Hollybush Rd BA12 19 E1
Holmbury Cl BA11 23 G4
Holme La BA13 15 B4
Holt Rd BA15 9 G3
Holyrood Cl BA14 12 C3
Home Cl BA14 13 E1
Homefield Ho BA12 19 F3
Honey La BA13 17 F6
Honeymans Cl BA14 11 F6
Honeysuckle Cl BA14 11 F6
Hoopers Barton BA11 3 A4
Hopgood Cl SN10 27 H1
Hopkins Rd SN10 27 G1
Hopton Ind Est SN10 27 G1
Hopton Rd SN10 27 G1
Hornbeam Cl BA11 23 F4
Hornbeam Cres SN12 7 F1
Horse Rd BA14 11 E2
Horton Av SN10 27 G1
Horton Cl BA15 9 G5
Horton Rd SN10 27 H1
Horton St BA11 22 B5
Hospital Rd BA13 17 G4
Houghton Cl BA12 19 G4
Houldsworth Av BA14 19 H2
Houston Way BA11 22 B5
Hungerford Av BA14 12 B1
Hunters Chase BA13 17 E4
Huntingdon Pl BA15 9 F2
Huntingdon Rise BA15 9 E1
Huntingdon St BA15 9 F1
Hurds Bldgs BA11 3 C6
Hurricane Rd SN12 7 E7
Hyde Rd BA14 10 D4

Jubilee Cl BA13 17 G3
Jubilee Ter BA13 22 C5
Jump Farm Rd SN10 27 F4
Junction Rd BA15 9 F3
Justice La BA11 3 B4

Katkins Alley BA11 3 B4
Keates Cl BA14 11 E4
Kemp Cl SN10 27 F4
Kempsfield SN10 25 E1
Kendrick Cl BA13 17 G3
Kenilworth Gdns SN12 7 C5
Kennedy Av SN12 4 F2
Kennet Cl,
  Melksham SN12 6 B2
Kennet Cl,
  Warminster BA12 18 D5
Kennet Gdns BA15 9 G3
Kennet Rd SN10 27 E6
Kennet Way BA14 11 E3
Kensington Cl BA14 11 E4
Kensington Flds BA14 12 B1
Kenton Dr BA14 11 F4
Kenwood Cl BA14 11 F6
Kestrel Cl SN12 7 D7
Kettle La BA14 13 H5
Ketton Cl BA14 10 A4
Kew Dr BA14 12 B1
Keyford BA11 3 B6
Keyford Cotts BA11 3 B6
Keyford Field Cotts BA11 24 C2
Keyford Gdns BA11 24 D1
Keyford Pl BA11 3 B6
Keyford Ter BA11 3 B6
Kiln Cl SN10 27 G5
King Alfred Way BA15 8 A2
King La BA12 18 C4
King St, Melksham SN12 6 C4
King St,
  Warminster BA12 18 C5
Kingfisher Dr,
  Devizes SN10 27 G2
Kingfisher Dr,
  Melksham SN12 7 E7
Kingfisher Dr,
  Westbury BA13 17 G2
Kings Ct BA12 18 C5
Kings Gdns BA14 11 E1
Kings Mead BA13 15 B3
Kings Rise BA12 18 C4
Kings St BA11 3 B4
Kingsbury Sq SN12 7 C5
Kingsdown Rd BA14 12 D3
Kingsfield BA15 9 G2
Kingsfield Cl BA15 9 G2
Kingsfield Grange Rd BA15 9 G2
Kingsley Gdns SN10 27 F5
Kingsley Pl BA14 10 A5
Kingsley Rd SN10 27 F4
Kingsmanor Wharf SN10 27 G2
Kingston Av BA15 9 G4
Kingston Rd BA15 9 F3
Kingswood Chase BA14 12 A2
Kirby Cl SN10 27 F3
Kitcheners Ct BA14 3 B1
Knights Cl BA11 3 B6
Knightstone Ct BA14 3 C2
Knightstone Heights BA11 3 C6

Laburnum Cl BA11 23 E3
Laburnum Dr SN12 7 B5
Laburnum Gro BA14 12 C2
Lacock Dr BA14 11 H4
Lacock Gdns BA14 11 H4
Ladydown BA14 10 D3
Lamb Ale Grn BA14 13 E1
Lamberts Marsh BA14 12 A6
Lambourn La BA13 15 E1
Lambourne Cres SN12 6 D4
Lambrok Cl BA14 12 A2
Lambrok Rd BA14 12 A1
Lancaster Pk Ind Est
  SN12 7 D7
Lancaster Rd SN12 7 D7
Langford Rd BA14 10 C4
Langholm Av BA12 18 B4
Langholm Cl BA12 18 B4
Langley Rd BA14 12 D3
Lanhams Cl BA13 17 G3
Lansdown Cl,
  Melksham SN12 6 E3
Lansdown Cl,
  Trowbridge BA14 12 C1
Lansdown Pl BA11 22 A5
Lansdowne Grn*,
  Sheep St SN10 27 E4
Lansdowne Ter*,
  Sheep St SN10 27 E4
Larch Cl SN12 7 B5
Larch Gro BA14 12 C2
Larchfield Cl BA11 23 E3
Larkdown BA14 11 F5
Larkspur BA14 11 F5
Late Broads BA15 8 A2
Laurel Cl BA11 23 F3
Laurel Gro BA14 12 D2
Lavender Cl,
  Melksham SN12 7 D5
Lavender Cl,
  Trowbridge BA14 13 F1

Lavender Ct BA11 23 E3
Laverton Cl BA13 17 G2
Laverton Grn BA13 17 F5
Laverton Rd BA13 17 F5
Lawrence Cl SN10 27 E6
Le Marchant Cl SN10 27 G2
Leafield Pl BA14 10 A5
Leap Gate BA14 11 G4
Leaze Cl BA11 22 B5
Leaze Rd, Frome BA11 22 B5
Leaze Rd,
  Melksham SN12 6 E2
Leigh Cl,
  Trowbridge BA14 13 E3
Leigh Cl, Westbury BA13 17 F4
Leigh Park Rd BA15 9 F1
Leigh Rd,
  Bradford-on-Avon BA15 9 G1
Leigh Rd,
  Trowbridge BA14 5 C1
Leigh Rd,
  Westbury BA13 17 F4
Leighton Grn BA13 17 G4
Leighton Home Farm Ct
  BA13 17 G4
Leighton La BA13 17 F4
Leighton Park Rd BA13 17 F5
Leighton Pk North BA13 17 F5
Leighton Pk West BA13 17 E5
Leonards Barton BA11 22 C4
Leslie Rise BA14 8 C6
Leversedge Rd BA11 22 D3
Lewis Cres BA14 22 D4
Lewis's Ct SN10 26 D4
Ley Rd BA13 17 E4
Leycroft Gdn BA11 22 D5
Leys Hill BA11 22 D4
Leys La BA11 22 D4
Leystone Cl BA11 22 D4
Liddington Way BA14 13 E3
Lilac Gro,
  Trowbridge BA14 12 C2
Lilac Gro, Westbury
  BA13 17 E3
Lilly Batch BA11 22 D3
Lime Av SN12 7 B5
Lime Cl BA11 23 E3
Lincoln Grn SN10 6 D2
Lincoln Gro SN12 7 E7
Linden Cl BA11 22 B5
Linden Cres BA15 8 C6
Linden Gro SN12 7 B5
Linden Pl BA14 3 A1
Linden Ter SN10 27 E4
Lindisfarne Cl BA15 8 B2
Link Rd BA13 14 B3
Linnet Way BA11 23 E4
Linsvale Cl BA11 23 F5
Linsvale Dr BA11 23 F5
Lion Pl SN12 4 A2
Lister Gro BA11 8 C6
Little Brittox SN10 26 D4
Little Common BA14 13 E5
Little Court La BA15 15 F1
Little Keyford La BA11 24 B4
Little London BA12 21 F5
Little Orchard BA12 18 D3
Little Pks BA14 5 E1
Littlejohn Av SN12 6 D2
Littleworth La SN12 4 E1
Lockeridge Cl BA14 13 E2
Locking Cl SN12 7 E8
Locks Hill BA11 3 C6
Loddon Way BA15 9 G4
Lodge Cl BA14 11 F6
London Rd SN10 27 E4
Long Grnd BA11 24 D1
Long Hollow BA13 15 F2
Long St SN10 26 D4
Longcroft Av SN10 27 F4
Longcroft Cres SN10 27 F4
Longcroft Rd SN10 27 F4
Longfield Rd BA14 4 C3
Longfields Walk SN10 27 E6
Longford Rd SN12 7 C5
Longlands BA13 15 D3
Longleat Cl BA11 24 C1
Longleat Rd BA11 3 A6
Longleaze La,
  Melksham SN12 7 D5
Longleaze La,
  Melksham SN12 7 E5
Lonsdale Gdns SN12 7 C6
Lopes Way BA13 17 F1
Lowbourne SN12 6 C4
Lower Alma St BA14 11 E6
Lower Bond Street Bldgs
  BA14 10 D1
Lower Ct BA14 10 D4
Lower Innox BA11 22 C3
Lower Keyford BA11 24 C1
Lower Marsh Rd BA12 11 F2
Lower Rd, Bratton BA13 15 A3
Lower Rd, Edington BA13 15 A2
Lower Westbury Rd BA13 15 A2
Lower Wharf SN10 26 C4
Lowmead BA14 11 E4
Loxley Cl SN10 27 F3
Ludlow Cl,
  Frome BA11 23 G4
Ludlow Cl,
  Warminster BA12 18 D5

Ludlow Cl,
  Westbury BA13 17 F1
Ludlow Hewitt Ct SN12 7 E7
Lullington La BA11 23 E1
Luxfield Rd BA12 18 C3
Lyddieth Ct BA15 8 A2
Lydiard Way BA14 13 E3
Lyes Gro BA13 16 C6
Lyme Av BA12 18 D4
Lyneham Way BA14 11 G5
Lynfield Rd BA11 22 B6
Lynwood Cl BA11 22 A6
Lynwood Dr BA14 10 A5
Lysander Rd SN12 7 D7

Maddocks Hill BA12 18 C5
Mafeking Ter BA11 3 A5
Magister Rd SN12 7 E7
Magnolia Cl BA11 23 F3
Magnolia Rise BA14 11 F6
Magnon Rd BA15 9 E2
Magpie Mws*,
  Bridewell St SN10 27 E5
Main St BA13 14 A4
Maismore Ter BA11 22 C5
Mallard Cl,
  Melksham SN12 7 E7
Mallard Cl,
  Westbury BA13 17 G2
Mallow Cl BA14 13 E2
Malthouse Ct BA14 24 C1
Malthouse Farm Cl SN12 6 E2
Malvern Cl,
  Melksham SN12 6 E4
Malvern Cl,
  Warminster BA12 19 E2
Manley Cl BA14 10 C5
Manor Cl BA14 12 B2
Manor Ct,
  Trowbridge BA14 12 B2
Manor Ct,
  Westbury BA13 15 D2
Manor Flds BA14 15 B4
Manor Furlong BA11 24 C2
Manor Gdns BA11 19 E3
Manor Rd, Frome BA11 24 C1
Manor Rd,
  Trowbridge BA14 12 B2
Manor Way BA11 24 C2
Mantles La BA12 21 G5
Manton Cl BA14 12 D2
Manvers St BA14 3 B1
Maple Cl SN12 6 E3
Maple Ct BA11 23 E4
Maple Gro BA14 12 D2
Maplecroft BA14 11 F5
Marden Walk BA14 13 E2
Margaret St SN12 6 B3
Marigold Cl SN12 7 D5
Marina Cl SN10 27 H1
Marina Dr BA14 10 D1
Maristow St BA13 17 G2
Market Pl, Devizes SN10 26 D4
Market Pl, Frome BA11 3 B4
Market Pl,
  Melksham SN12 6 C4
Market Pl,
  Warminster BA12 19 E3
Market Pl,
  Westbury BA13 17 G2
Market St,
  Bradford-on-Avon BA15 9 F2
Market St,
  Trowbridge BA14 3 C2
Marsh Rd BA14 11 E1
Marsh St BA14 18 D5
Marshall Rd SN10 27 E4
Marshmead BA14 11 F2
Marston Cl BA14 24 B2
Marston La BA11 24 B2
Marston Mead BA11 24 B2
Marston Pk Ind Est
  BA11 24 A4
Marston Rd, Frome BA11 24 B2
Marston Rd,
  Trowbridge BA14 12 C3
Marston Trading Est
  BA11 24 C2
Marti Cl SN12 6 D4
Martigny Ct SN12 7 D5
Martigny Rd SN12 7 D5
Martin Crest BA12 18 C5
Maryport St SN10 26 D4
Masefield Rd BA12 18 B3
Maslen Cl SN10 27 G4
Masons La BA15 9 F2
Masons Way BA11 24 B2
Massey Rd SN10 27 F6
Matilda Way SN10 27 F3
Matravers Cl BA13 17 F3
Matt La BA14 13 G5
Matthew Ley Cl BA13 17 F4
Mattock Cl SN10 27 F4
Maud Cl SN10 27 F3
Maulton Cl BA14 5 D2
Maxcroft La BA14 11 E1
Mayenne Pl SN10 26 A4
Maytree Cl BA11 23 F3
Mead Pk SN12 4 B2
Meadow Dr BA13 17 F2

Meadow Dr SN10 27 F
Meadow La BA13 17 F
Meadow Rd,
  Frome BA11 22 D
Meadow Rd,
  Melksham SN12 6 D
Meadowfield BA15 8 D
Meads Pl SN10 27 E
Meadway BA14 10 A
Medleys Cotts SN12 4 A
Melbourne St BA13 15 B
Melksham Trading Est
  SN12 18 C
Melrose Av BA12 18 C
Melrose Cl BA12 18 C
Melton Rd BA13 10 D
Mendip Cl, Frome BA11 22 D
Mendip Cl,
  Melksham SN12 6 E
Mendip Dr,
  Warminster BA12 19 E
Mendip Dr BA11 22 D
Mendip Gdns BA11 23 F
Merchants Barton Ind Est
  BA11 3 C
Meridian Walk BA14 10 B
Merlin Cl BA13 17 G
Merlin Way SN12 7 D
Methuen Av SN12 6 D
Methuen Cl BA15 9 G
Middle Ct BA14 11 F
Middle La,
  Melksham SN12 4 F
Middle La,
  Trowbridge BA14 11 F
Middle Rank BA15 9 F
Middlefield Cl SN10 27 F
Middleton Ct BA14 18 C
Midlands Ind Est BA14 3 D
Milbourn Cl BA15 8 A
Milk St BA11 3 B
Mill Cl, Devizes SN10 27 F
Mill Cl, Frome BA11 22 C
Mill La,
  Bishopstrow BA12 20 B
Mill La,
  Bradford-on-Avon BA15 9 F
Mill La,
  Hawkeridge BA13 14 C
Mill La,
  Heytesbury BA12 21 G
Mill La, Trowbridge BA14 3 A
Mill La, Westbury BA13 16 D
Mill Rd, Devizes SN10
Mill Rd, Potterne SN10 25 A
Mill St, Trowbridge BA14 3 A
Mill St,
  Warminster BA12 19 G
Millennium Cl SN10 27 G
Millhand Villas BA14 13 F
Millington Dr BA14 10 B
Mills Rd SN12 6 E
Milton Av SN12 18 C
Minster Vw BA12 18 C
Mitchell Dr SN12 7 E
Moat Rd BA13 14 B
Monastery Rd BA13 15 D
Monday Market St SN10 26 D
Monmouth Dr BA11 23 E
Montague Ct BA14 11 G
Montague Pl SN12 6 B
Moonrakers SN10 27 F
Morgan Walk BA13 17 E
Morgans La BA11 3 A
Morley Fld BA12 19 G
Morris La SN10 26 D
Mortimer St BA14 9 F
Moulton Dr BA15 9 F
Mount La BA12 18 D
Mount Pleasant,
  Bradford-on-Avon BA15 9 F
Mount Pleasant,
  Frome BA11 24 D
Mount Pleasant,
  Melksham SN12 4 C
Mounts Fld BA11 24 D
Moyle Pk BA14 11 G
Moyne Cl SN10 26 C
Mulberry Cl BA11 23 E
Murray Rd BA14 10 D
Murray Walk SN12 6 D
Myrtle Av BA12 18 D
Mythern Mdw BA15 9 G

Naishs St BA11 3 A
Naughton Av SN10 27 G
Navigator Cl BA14 11 E
Neate Rd SN10 27 F
New Bldgs BA11 24 D
New Broughton Rd SN12 6 E
New Buildings La BA11 24 D
New Lawns SN12 6 C
New Park Rd SN10 26 D
New Park St SN10 26 D
New Rd,
  Bradford-on-Avon BA15 9 F
New Rd, Melksham SN12 6 E
New Rd, Trowbridge BA14 3 B
New Ter BA14 5 E
Newhurst Pk BA14 11 G
Newington Cl BA11 23 F

ewington Ter BA11 3 B6
ewleaze BA14 11 G2
ewmarket Av BA14 13 F4
ewopaul Way BA12 18 D1
ewport BA12 19 E2
ewtown,
Bradford-on-Avon BA15 9 E3
ewtown,
Trowbridge BA14 3 A2
ewtown,
Warminster BA12 21 G5
ewtown,
Westbury BA13 17 H2
ightingale Av BA11 23 E3
ightingale Dr BA13 17 G2
ightingale Rd BA14 10 B6
orleaze BA13 14 D2
orridge Vw BA12 18 C3
orrington La SN12 4 E4
orris Rd BA14 11 H3
orth La BA12 18 B3
orth Par BA11 3 C4
orth Row BA12 19 E3
Northacre Ind Pk BA13 14 A4
orthbrook Rd SN12 6 A1
orthcote Cres BA11 23 E3
orthfield BA15 8 B2
orthgate Gdns SN10 26 C4
orthgate St SN10 26 C4
orton Rd BA12 20 B6
orton Ct SN12 6 B3
unney Rd BA11 3 A5
ursery Cl,
Melksham SN12 4 A3
ursery Cl,
Trowbridge BA14 11 G3
ursteed Cl SN10 27 F6
Nursteed Ind Est SN10 27 F6
ursteed Pk SN10 27 F6
ursteed Rd SN10 27 E4
Nursteed Trading Est
SN10 27 G6

ak Dr BA14 12 D5
ak Tree Cl BA11 10 B5
akfield Cl BA11 22 A5
akfield Rd BA11 22 A5
akwood Dr SN12 6 C4
amaru Way SN10 27 F4
ffers Ct SN10 27 E4
l Gormans Mws SN12 6 E2
ld Broughton Rd SN12 6 B3
ld Dilton Rd BA13 17 F6
ldfield Pk BA13 17 E2
ldfield Rd BA13 17 E3
rchard Cl,
Bradford-on-Avon BA15 8 C6
rchard Cl, Devizes SN10 26 D6
rchard Cl, Frome BA11 22 A6
rchard Ct,
Warminster BA12 19 F2
rchard Ct,
Westbury BA13 16 C6
rchard Ct,
Trowbridge BA14 13 E1
rchard Ct,
Westbury BA13 17 G3
rchard Dr BA14 12 A5
rchard Gdns,
Bradford-on-Avon BA15 9 F3
rchard Gdns,
Melksham SN12 7 C5
rchard Leigh Vw BA11 22 B5
rchard Rd,
Trowbridge BA14 13 E1
rchard Rd,
Westbury BA13 17 G3
rchard St BA11 3 A4
rchard Vw BA14 12 D5
riel Cl BA14 11 G2
rpington Way BA14 11 H5
sborne Rd BA14 11 F3
sprey Cl SN12 7 E7
ver Innox BA11 22 C4

ack Saddle Way BA11 22 C3
anfield Gdns SN12 7 A7
ainters Mead BA14 11 G4
alairet Cl BA15 9 G5
almer Dr BA15 9 G1
almer Rd BA14 10 D4
almer St BA11 3 B5
ampas Ct BA12 18 C3
ans La SN10 27 E5
ark Cl BA14 13 E5
ark Hill Dr BA11 22 D4
ark La,
Warminster BA12 21 H6
ark La, Westbury BA13 14 F3
ark Rd, Frome BA11 3 A5
ark Rd, Trowbridge BA14 3 C2
ark St, Trowbridge BA14 16 B6
ark St, Trowbridge BA14 3 A3
ark St,
Warminster BA12 21 G5
ark Vw SN10 26 B4
arkfields SN10 27 F2
arklands BA14 10 D3
arkview Dr BA13 17 F3
arsonage La BA13 15 D2
arsonage Rd BA14 11 G5

Paul St BA11 3 B5
Paveley Cl BA13 17 E2
Pavely Gdns BA14 11 G5
Paxcroft Way BA14 11 F5
Pear Tree Cl SN12 4 E2
Pear Tree Orchard BA13 15 B3
Pecheron Pl BA13 17 E3
Pedlars Gro BA11 22 C3
Pegasus Way SN12 7 D7
Pembroke Cl BA13 13 E2
Pembroke Rd SN12 6 D4
Penleigh Rd BA13 17 E3
Pennine Cl BA11 6 E4
Pennycress Dr SN12 7 D5
Pennyfarthing Row BA13 17 E5
Pennys Piece BA13 23 H4
Pensford Way BA11 23 G3
Penwood Cl BA13 17 E2
Pepper Pl BA12 19 G2
Pepperacre La BA14 11 F4
Perretts Ct SN12 6 C4
Perriwinkle Cl BA12 18 B3
Peto Gro BA15 8 C6
Petticoat La SN10 16 C6
Philip Cl SN12 6 D2
Phillip Cl SN10 27 F3
Phipps Cl BA13 17 F1
Phoenix Rise BA13 17 E2
Pine Cl BA11 7 B5
Pine Ct BA11 23 E3
Pine Walk BA14 12 D5
Pines Rd SN10 27 F5
Pinmore BA11 24 D2
Pintail Way BA11 17 G2
Piplar Grnd BA15 9 F5
Pit Mead La BA12 20 A3
Pitman Av BA14 12 C1
Pitman Ct BA14 12 C1
Place Rd SN12 6 C4
Plane Tree Cl SN12 4 E2
Plants Grn BA12 19 F4
Polebarn Rd BA14 3 D1
Poplar Cl BA11 23 E3
Port Way BA13 15 A4
Portland Pl BA11 22 B5
Portland Rd BA11 22 B5
Portman Rd BA11 6 B2
Portway, Frome BA11 3 C6
Portway,
Warminster BA12 19 E3
Portway La BA12 19 E2
Portway Mws BA12 19 E2
Post Office La SN12 4 B2
Poston Way BA15 8 A2
Pot La BA3 23 H1
Potterne Rd SN10 26 D6
Poulsen Cl BA12 19 E4
Poulton BA15 9 F4
Poulton La BA15 9 G5
Pound Barton Ind Est
BA12 20 B5
Pound Cl BA14 18 C4
Pound Farm Cl BA14 11 F2
Pound La BA15 9 F3
Pound Row BA14 18 C3
Pound St BA12 18 C4
Prestbury Dr BA12 19 F4
Priddy Cl BA11 23 G3
Primrose Dr SN12 6 E4
Primrose Walk BA12 18 C3
Prince Maurice Ct SN10 27 G2
Princecroft La BA12 18 C4
Princess Anne Rd BA11 23 E3
Princess Gdns,
Trowbridge BA14 11 E1
Princess Gdns,
Warminster BA12 19 H4
Priory Cl BA15 9 F2
Priory Pk BA15 9 F2
Proby Pl BA14 11 G5
Prospect Flds SN12 4 B3
Prospect Pl BA14 10 D4
Prospect Sq BA13 17 G3
Proudman Rd SN10 27 F3
Purlpit SN12 4 C2

Quakers Walk SN10 26 D3
Quantock Cl,
Melksham SN12 6 E4
Quantock Cl,
Warminster BA12 19 E1
Quarry Cl SN10 27 F4
Quartermaster Rd BA13 14 B4
Quarterway La BA14 11 E5
Queens Club Gdns BA14 10 A5
Queens Gdns BA14 11 E1
Queens Rd,
Devizes SN10 26 D5
Queens Rd, Frome BA11 22 B6
Queens Rd,
Trowbridge BA14 10 D4
Queens Rd,
Westbury BA13 17 E3
Queens Road App BA13 3 A5
Queens Sqa BA13 17 E2
Queensway,
Melksham SN12 6 D3
Queensway,
Warminster BA12 19 H4
Quilling SN10 13 F1

Radnor Cl SN10 27 E6
Radnor Pl SN12 7 C5
Ragleth Gro BA14 11 F4
Raleigh Cl BA14 3 D2
Rambler Cl BA14 10 B5
Ramsbury Walk BA14 13 E2
Randolph Rd BA11 6 C4
Ravenscroft Gdns BA14 11 F4
Rectory Cl BA12 19 E2
Red Hat La BA14 3 C1
Red Pit BA13 16 A6
Redgrave Cl BA14 13 E2
Redhorn Gdns SN10 27 E6
Redland La BA13 17 F3
Redlands BA13 15 B3
Reed Cl SN10 27 F4
Reeves Rd SN10 27 F6
Regal Ct BA12 19 E3
Regents Pl,
Bradford-on-Avon BA15 9 F4
Regents Pl,
Trowbridge BA14 12 B2
Rendells Ct SN10 26 D4
Richmond Cl,
Devizes SN10 27 H1
Richmond Cl,
Trowbridge BA14 10 B6
Richmond Rd BA11 24 C1
Rickfield BA15 9 E3
Rider Cl SN10 27 H1
River Cl BA15 9 F3
Rivers Reach BA11 3 A4
Riverside Dr SN12 6 C2
Riverway BA14 3 A1
Riverway Ind Est BA14 3 A1
Robin Cl BA12 19 F3
Robins La BA14 22 B5
Rocher Cl BA13 17 F3
Rock La BA12 19 G4
Rock Rd BA14 12 C1
Rodden La BA11 23 E6
Rodden Rd BA11 3 D4
Roddenbury Cl BA11 23 E5
Rodwell Pk BA14 11 E4
Rook La BA11 3 B5
Rookes La SN10 25 B4
Rooks La BA11 23 H4
Rope Walk SN10 27 E4
Rosebrook Gdns SN12 7 D5
Rosedale Gdns BA14 10 A5
Rosedale Walk BA11 22 D4
Rosefield Way BA13 17 F2
Roseland Av SN10 27 E5
Roseland Av SN10 27 E5
Rosemary Steps BA15 9 F2
Rosemary Walk BA11 9 F3
Rosenheim Rise BA13 15 A3
Rossett Gdns BA14 10 B6
Rossiters Hill BA11 24 C1
Rossiters Rd BA11 24 C1
Rothe Rise BA13 17 F5
Rotherstone SN10 26 D3
Roundponds SN12 6 A2
Roundstone St BA14 3 C1
Roundway Gdns SN10 27 E2
Roundway Pk SN10 27 E2
Rowan Ct, Frome BA11 23 E3
Rowan Ct,
Melksham SN12 7 B5
Rowden La BA15 9 F5
Rowley Pl SN12 6 D4
Royal Oak Ct SN10 26 D4
Rupert Cl SN10 27 H1
Ruskin Av SN12 6 D4
Ruskin Dr BA12 18 B4
Russett Ct BA12 18 B3
Rutland Cl SN12 7 D5
Rutland Cres BA14 12 D1
Ryeland Way BA14 13 F1
Ryeleaze SN10 27 F4

St Aldhelm Rd BA15 9 G4
St Aldhelms Cl BA11 22 B6
St Andrews Rd,
Melksham SN12 6 D3
St Andrews Rd,
Warminster BA12 18 B4
St Annes Cl BA14 12 B4
St Athan Cl SN12 7 E8
St Augustines Rd BA14 10 B6
St Bridget Cl SN10 27 G4
St Devizes Rd SN10 26 A2
St Georges Cl BA12 20 A1
St Georges Ter BA14 3 B2
St Johns Cres BA14 12 A2
St Johns Cl SN10 26 D4
St Johns Rd,
Frome BA11 23 E5
St Johns Rd,
Warminster BA12 19 G4
St Johns St SN10 26 D4
St Josephs La SN10 26 C4
St Katherines Quay BA15 9 F4
St Laurence Rd BA15 9 G4
St Margarets Cl BA14 12 B2
St Margarets Gdns SN12 6 D3
St Margarets Hill BA15 9 F3
St Margarets St BA15 9 F3
St Margarets Steps BA15 9 F3
St Margarets Villas BA15 9 F3
St Marys Cl,
Devizes SN10 25 B3

St Marys Cl,
Trowbridge BA14 11 F1
St Marys Gdns BA14 11 E2
St Marys La BA13 16 B5
St Marys Rd BA11 23 E5
St Michaels Cl BA14 11 G3
St Michaels Rd SN12 7 B5
St Nicholas Cl,
Bradford-on-Avon BA15 8 A2
St Nicholas Cl,
Trowbridge BA14 13 E5
St Stephens Pl BA14 3 C2
St Thomas Pass BA14 10 D5
St Thomas Rd BA14 11 E5
Salisbury Cl BA13 3 C2
Salisbury Hollow BA15 15 F2
Salisbury St SN10 26 B4
Salisbury Ter BA11 24 C1
Sambourne Chase BA12 18 D3
Sambourne Gdns BA12 19 E3
Sambourne Rd BA12 18 D4
Sand Cl BA15 9 G2
Sanders Rd SN10 10 D4
Sandfield BA12 20 B6
Sandhole La BA13 17 E5
Sandown Centre BA14 13 F4
Sandridge Rd SN12 6 D3
Sandringham Rd BA14 12 C3
Sandy Leaze SN12 9 E3
Sandys Hill La BA11 24 B3
Sangster Av SN12 6 D4
Sarum Av SN12 7 C6
Sarum Dr SN10 27 E6
Sarum Gdns BA13 17 G1
Sassoon Cl BA12 18 B4
Savernake Av SN12 6 E2
Savernake Cl BA12 19 E2
Saxifrage Bank SN12 7 E5
Saxon Cl BA13 17 F2
Saxon Dr BA14 11 E1
Saxon Way BA15 8 B2
Saxons Acre BA12 18 B3
Saxonvale BA11 3 B4
School La,
Trowbridge BA14 5 C4
School La,
Westbury BA13 17 E5
School Lane Cl BA14 10 D1
Scotland Rd SN12 6 B2
Scott Rd BA11 3 B4
Sedge Mead BA11 22 D3
Sedgefield Gdns SN10 27 E4
Selwood Cres BA11 22 D3
Selwood Rd BA11 3 A4
Semington Rd BA14 7 B8
Severn Rd SN12 6 C2
Seymour Cl SN10 10 C5
Seymour Rd BA14 10 D5
Shackleton Rd SN10 27 F5
Shaftesbury Ct BA14 12 B2
Shails La BA14 3 B1
Shails La BA14 10 C5
Shaw Hill SN10 4 F3
Shearman St BA14 13 E1
Sheep St SN10 27 E4
Sheepcote Barton BA14 13 E1
Shell Cl SN12 6 D3
Shelley Gdns SN12 6 C4
Shelley Way BA12 18 B4
Shepherds Mead BA13 16 A6
Sheppard Cl SN10 26 C3
Sheppards Barton BA11 3 B5
Sherborne Rd BA14 10 D4
Sheridan Gdns BA14 12 A2
Sherwood Av SN10 6 E2
Sherwood Cl BA12 19 E2
Shetland Cl BA14 17 E4
Shire Way BA13 17 E4
Shore Pl BA14 10 A5
Shoreland Cl BA13 17 F3
Short St SN12 6 E2
Shoscombe Gdn BA11 23 F3
Shrewton Cl BA14 13 E2
Shurnhold SN12 6 A1
Sidmouth St SN10 27 E4
Silbury Cl BA11 17 F2
Silver Birch Gro BA14 12 C3
Silver Mdws BA14 12 B3
Silver St,
Bradford-on-Avon BA15 9 G4
Silver St, Devizes SN10 25 B3
Silver St,
Trowbridge BA14 3 C2
Silver St,
Warminster BA12 18 D3
Silver St, Westbury BA13 16 C5
Silver Street La BA14 12 B2
Singers Cl BA11 22 C5
Singers Knoll BA11 3 C6
Sladesbrook BA15 9 G3
Sladesbrook Cl BA15 9 G1
Slag La BA13 17 E1
Sleight Cotts SN10 25 F2
Sleight La SN10 25 F2
Slowgrove Cl BA14 11 F6
Smallbrook Gdns BA11 11 E1
Smallbrook La BA12 19 G5
Smallbrook Rd BA12 19 F5
Smithwell Cl BA14 11 F5
Snails La SN10 26 C4
Snappersnipes BA13 17 G3

Snarlton La SN12 6 E3
Snowberry La SN12 7 D5
Snowy Ter SN10 27 E4
Snuff St SN10 26 D4
Somerset Cres SN12 7 D5
Somerset Dr BA13 17 G1
Somerset Rd BA11 3 A5
Somerton Gdns BA11 23 F3
Sorrell Cl,
Melksham SN12 7 D5
Sorrell Cl,
Trowbridge BA14 13 E2
South Par BA11 3 A5
South St BA12 18 C5
South View Rd BA14 13 E2
Southay BA13 15 B4
Southbrook Rd SN12 6 B2
Southbroom Rd SN10 27 E5
Southfield BA14 12 A6
Southfields BA11 24 D1
Southgate SN10 26 D5
Southgate Cl SN10 27 E5
Southleigh BA15 9 E4
Southleigh Vw BA12 19 F4
Southville BA15 9 H4
Southville Rd BA15 9 G4
Southway BA14 13 E1
Southway Rd BA15 9 F5
Southwick Rd BA14 12 D6
Southwood Rd BA14 11 F6
Spa Ct SN12 7 C5
Spa Rd BA11 3 C4
Sparnick La BA13 17 E5
Speedwell Cl,
Melksham SN12 7 D6
Speedwell Cl,
Trowbridge BA14 13 E2
Speer Ct SN10 25 D1
Spencer Cl SN12 6 B2
Spencers Orchard BA15 9 F5
Spinners Cft BA14 13 E1
Spring Mdws BA14 12 B3
Spring Rd BA11 22 D4
Springers Cl SN10 27 F4
Springfield BA15 9 G3
Springfield Cl BA14 11 E4
Springfield Gdns SN12 4 F2
Springfield Pl BA14 17 F4
Springfield Rd BA13 17 F4
Stallard St BA14 3 A2
Stancomb Av BA14 11 E4
Stanford Ct*,
Sheep St SN10 27 E4
Stanier Cl BA11 23 G4
Stanley Ter BA11 27 E5
Stanton Cl BA14 13 E2
Starfield Ct BA14 5 E2
Station App, Frome BA11 3 D6
Station App,
Melksham SN12 7 E1
Station App,
Westbury BA13 17 E1
Station Rd, Devizes SN10 26 C4
Station Rd,
Trowbridge BA14 5 E1
Station Rd,
Warminster BA12 19 F3
Station Rd,
Westbury BA13 17 E1
Station Way BA14 3 B2
Staverton Rd BA14 5 C3
Steele Cl SN10 27 F4
Stephens Way BA12 18 D1
Stephenson Dr BA11 23 G4
Sterling Cl SN12 7 D7
Stevens La BA11 24 C1
Stillman Cl BA14 5 D1
Stirling Way BA11 23 F4
Stockwell Rd SN10 27 F3
Stokehill BA14 11 G5
Stokes Cl SN10 27 H1
Stonebridge Dr BA11 23 E3
Stonefield Cl BA15 9 G4
Stonelea BA14 11 G3
Stoneleigh Rise BA11 22 D4
Stonewall Ter BA11 24 D2
Stony St BA11 3 B5
Stormore BA13 16 A6
Storridge Rd BA13 14 A3
Stourton Cl BA11 24 B1
Stourton Gdns BA11 24 B1
Stourton Pk BA11 11 H3
Stourton Vw BA11 24 B1
Stradbrook BA13 15 C3
Strattons Walk SN12 6 C4
Stroud La SN10 25 D4
Stuart Cl BA14 11 E2
Stuart Grn BA12 19 E4
Studland Pk BA13 17 G4
Studley Farm La BA14 4 B3
Studley Rise BA14 13 E2
Styles Av BA11 23 F6
Styles Cl BA11 23 F6
Styles Hill BA11 23 F6
Styles Mdw BA11 23 F6
Styles Pk BA11 23 F6
Summer Hill BA11 23 F6
Summer Rd BA13 17 F2
Summerdown Ct BA13 17 G3
Summerdown Walk BA14 12 D3
Summerleaze BA14 12 B2

Sun La BA13 17 E5
Sun St BA11 3 A4
Sunderland Cl SN12 7 E8
Sunnyside BA11 24 D1
Sunnyside Pl BA11 24 D1
Surrey Pl BA14 12 D1
Sussex Wharf SN10 26 C4
Sutton Cl BA13 23 F3
Sutton Pl SN10 27 E5
Swallow Cl BA12 18 C5
Swallow Dr, Frome BA11 23 F4
Swallow Dr,
 Trowbridge BA14 10 B6
Swan Dr BA14 10 D1
Sweetbriar Rd SN12 7 D5
Swift Mead BA12 18 C5
Sycamore Dr BA11 23 F3
Sycamore Gro,
 Trowbridge BA14 12 C2
Sycamore Gro,
 Westbury BA13 17 E3

Talbot Cl SN12 6 E3
Talbot Rd BA14 12 B1
Tamar Rd SN12 6 C2
Tangmere Cl SN12 7 E8
Tanis SN10 26 A1
Tankeys Cl BA11 22 D3
Tascroft BA12 18 A5
Taylors Vw BA14 3 D1
Teal Cl BA13 17 G1
Teddington Ct BA12 18 D3
Teeside BA14 12 A5
Teichman Cl BA12 19 F4
Tennyson Cl BA12 18 C4
Thackeray Cres SN12 6 C4
Thames Cl BA12 19 E5
Thames Cres SN12 6 B2
The Ark SN10 26 D5
The Avenue,
 Dilton Marsh BA13 16 B6
The Avenue,
 Warminster BA12 19 E3
The Avenue,
 Westbury BA13 17 F3
The Ball BA13 15 B4
The Beeches,
 Melksham SN12 4 F3
The Beeches,
 Trowbridge BA14 11 F4
The Beeches,
 Warminster BA12 18 D4
The Blue Ho BA11 3 B4
The Breach SN10 26 D5
The Brittox SN10 26 D4
The Butts, Bratton BA13 15 E2
The Butts, Devizes SN10 25 B4
The Butts, Frome BA11 3 A6
The Butts, Westbury BA13 17 G4
The Circle BA13 16 B6
The City, Melksham SN12 7 C5
The City, Westbury BA13 17 E3
The Close,
 Melksham SN12 7 C5
The Close,
 Warminster BA12 19 E3
The Common BA14 5 E1
The Cooperage BA11 3 B6
The Copse BA11 3 A6
The Corn Market BA12 19 E3
The Crays SN12 6 D3
The Crescent,
 Dilton Marsh BA13 16 B6
The Crescent,
 Westbury BA13 17 F3
The Croft,
 Bradford-on-Avon BA15 8 C6
The Croft, Devizes SN10 27 F4
The Croft,
 Trowbridge BA14 12 D2
The Dene BA12 20 A1
The Down BA14 11 F4
The Downlands BA12 19 F2
The Elms,
 Bradford-on-Avon BA15 9 E1
The Elms,
 Trowbridge BA14 5 D1
The Fairway SN10 26 D6
The Friars SN12 6 D2
The Gravel BA14 5 E1
The Grove, Frome BA11 24 B2
The Grove,
 Warminster BA12 19 E3
The Halve BA14 3 D1
The Heathlands BA12 18 C5
The Hollow BA13 16 C6
The Homelands BA12 18 C4
The Knap BA14 11 G3
The Knoll BA13 17 H1
The Laurels BA15 8 C6
The Maltings,
 Bradford-on-Avon BA15 9 F4

The Maltings, Frome BA11 3 B5
The Maltings,
 Warminster BA12 18 D3
The Market Pl SN10 26 D4
The Mead,
 Bradford-on-Avon BA15 8 B2
The Mead,
 Warminster BA12 19 E2
The Mead,
 Westbury BA13 17 F1
The Mews BA14 19 E3
The Midlands BA14 5 D1
The Mill Ho BA15 9 G3
The Mint BA11 3 A4
The Moorlands SN10 26 C5
The Mount, Frome BA11 24 D2
The Mount,
 Trowbridge BA14 11 E4
The Nestings BA14 12 B3
The Nursery SN10 26 C3
The Oaks BA12 19 E1
The Old Batch BA15 9 E1
The Paddock BA13 19 F4
The Paddocks BA11 11 F5
The Pastures BA15 8 B6
The Patchway SN10 27 G4
The Picquet BA13 15 B4
The Pippins BA12 18 D3
The Poplars BA14 12 B3
The Rank BA14 12 D5
The Retreat BA11 23 E6
The Ridgeway BA12 13 F5
The Shambles BA15 9 F2
The Shires Shopping Centre
BA14 3 B1
The Sidings SN10 26 C4
The Slipway BA14 10 D1
The Spitfire Retail Pk
BA14 13 E3
The Square BA14 5 C4
The Stables BA15 17 G3
The Star BA13 5 D2
The Street BA14 5 D2
The Teasels BA13 18 D3
The Tynings BA13 17 F4
The Uplands BA12 19 F2
The Village Grn BA13 14 E2
The Walk BA14 5 D2
The Weir BA13 15 E2
The Wilderness BA15 9 F2
The Woodlands BA12 19 E1
Thestfield Dr BA14 10 D2
Thorn Leigh SN12 6 C4
Thornbank SN12 7 C5
Thornbury Rd BA14 17 F2
Thornhill Rd BA12 18 B5
Three Lions Mws BA14 5 D2
Thurnham Ct SN10 25 D1
Tickle Belly La BA13 17 F5
Tilley Cl SN10 27 F4
Timbrell St BA14 10 D5
Timor Rd BA13 15 E1
Tinhead Rd BA13 15 E1
Tintern Rd SN10 27 E6
Tollbar Cl SN10 25 B3
Top La SN12 4 E2
Tor Ho BA13 17 F2
Torino Cl SN10 27 F3
Tory BA15 9 E3
Tory Pl BA15 9 E3
Tower Cl BA14 12 B1
Tower Hill BA13 16 D6
Tower Rd SN10 6 E3
Tower Vw BA11 24 D2
Town Bri BA14 3 B1
Townsend Fm SN12 7 B8
Towpath Rd BA14 11 E1

Treenwood Ind Est
BA15 9 F5
Trenchard Way SN10 7 D7
Trent Cres SN12 6 C2
Trevithick Cl BA13 23 G4
Trinity Row BA11 3 A4
Trinity St BA11 3 A4
Trinity Walk BA11 3 A4
Trowbridge Lodge
 Residential Pk BA14 11 F6
Trowbridge Rd,
 Bradford-on-Avon BA15 9 F3
Trowbridge Rd,
 Bratton BA13 15 A2
Trowbridge Rd,
 Trowbridge BA14 11 G4
Trowbridge Rd,
 Westbury BA13 17 G1
Trowle BA14 10 A3
Tudor Dr BA14 11 E1
Tyning Cl SN10 27 E5
Tyning La BA13 15 B4
Tyning Rd BA15 8 B2

Tynings Way BA15 8 B6
Tytherington Rd BA12 21 G5

Union St,
 Melksham SN12 6 C4
Union St,
 Trowbridge BA14 3 C1
Upland Rise BA13 17 G3
Upper Broad St BA14 3 B1
Upper Garston La BA13 15 B4
Upper Marsh Rd BA14 19 E4
Upper Mill BA15 9 G3
Upper Regents Pk BA15 9 F3
Upper Westwood BA15 8 A6
Upper Whatcombe BA11 22 B4
Upton Cl BA12 18 C3

Valentia Ct SN12 7 E7
Valiant Cl SN12 7 E7
Valley Vw BA11 22 B4
Vallis Mills Trading Est
BA11 22 A5
Vallis Rd BA11 3 A4
Vallis Vw BA11 3 A4
Vernal La BA11 22 B4
Vicarage St, Frome BA11 3 B5
Vicarage St,
 Warminster BA12 18 D3
Victoria Gdns BA14 11 F3
Victoria Mws BA12 18 C3
Victoria Rd,
 Devizes SN10 27 E3
Victoria Rd, Frome BA11 3 D6
Victoria Rd,
 Trowbridge BA14 11 E3
Victoria Rd,
 Warminster BA12 18 A4
Victory Rd BA14 14 A3
Vincent Cl SN12 6 E4
Vine Cotts BA15 9 E2
Vine Gdns BA11 22 C4
Viney La BA11 24 C4
Virginia Dr BA12 18 B3
Vista BA13 17 G3

Waiblingen Way SN10 26 C3
Wainwright Dr BA11 23 G3
Walden Lodge Cl SN10 27 E6
Walker Rd BA11 24 D1
Wallbridge BA11 23 E6
Wallbridge Av BA11 3 D6
Wallbridge Gdns BA11 3 D5
Wallis Cl SN12 7 E8
Walmesley Chase BA14 11 G5
Walnut Cl BA12 20 B6
Walnut Gro BA14 12 C2
Walnut Wlk BA11 23 E2
Warbler Cl BA14 10 B6
Warburton Cl BA14 12 C2
Wardour Pl SN12 7 C6
Warleigh Cl BA11 22 A6
Warminster Rd BA13 17 F5
Warwick Cres SN12 7 C5
Washington Rd BA13 14 A4
Water La BA11 3 A6
Waterford Beck BA14 12 A1
Waterloo BA11 3 B4
Waterside Pk SN10 27 H2
Watermead BA13 17 G2
Waterworks Rd BA14 12 C1
Watery La BA12 20 A3
Waverley Cl BA11 23 G4
Waverley Gdns SN12 7 C5
Waylands SN10 27 F5
Wayside Cl BA14 23 F4
Weavers Cft SN12 6 B3
Weavers Ct BA11 24 B1
Weavers Dr BA14 13 E1
Webbers St BA14 12 B2
Wedmore Cl BA14 23 F3
Weirside St BA13 15 E2
Weirside Mill BA15 9 G3
Wellesley Cl SN12 7 E8
Wellhead La BA13 17 F4
Wellington Dr SN12 7 E7
Wellington Sq SN12 7 E6
Wellow Dr BA14 23 F3
Welshmill La BA11 22 C5
Welshmill Rd BA11 3 C4
Were Cl BA12 18 C3
Wesley Cl, Frome BA11 3 B5
Wesley Cl,
 Trowbridge BA14 12 A6
Wesley La BA14 12 A6
Wesley Rd BA14 3 A3
Wesley Slope BA11 3 A3
Wessex Cl, Devizes SN10 27 F4
Wessex Cl,
 Melksham SN12 7 D5
Wessex Flds BA11 24 B2
Wessex Walk BA13 17 F2
West Ashton Rd BA14 13 D2

West End,
 Melksham SN12 7 C5
West End,
 Westbury BA13 17 G2
West Hill SN12 4 D2
West Par BA12 18 D4
West St, Trowbridge BA14 3 A2
West St,
 Warminster BA12 18 C3
West Street Pl BA12 18 C3
West View Cres BA11 22 D5

West Wiltshire Trading Est
BA13 14 A3
Westbourne Gdns BA14 3 A2
Westbourne Rd,
 Trowbridge BA14 3 A3
Westbourne Rd,
 Westbury BA13 17 G3
Westbury BA13 17 E1
Westbury Ind Est BA11 17 E1
Westbury Leigh BA13 16 D6
Westbury Rd,
 Bratton BA13 15 A4
Westbury Rd,
 Heywood BA13 14 E1
Westbury Rd,
 Trowbridge BA14 13 E5
Westbury Rd,
 Warminster BA12 19 E1
Westbury Vw BA14 9 E4
Westcott Cl BA11 23 G4
Westcroft St BA14 10 C4
Western Way SN12 6 B4
Westfield BA15 9 E2
Westfield Cl BA14 12 B1
Westfield Rd,
 Frome BA11 22 B6
Westfield Rd,
 Trowbridge BA14 12 B1
Westlands BA12 21 F5
Westleigh BA12 18 C3
Westmead Cres BA14 12 C3
Westover BA11 22 A6
Westridge SN10 26 D4
Westwood Dr BA11 22 A6
Westwood Rd,
 Bradford-on-Avon BA15 8 D6
Westwood Rd,
 Trowbridge BA14 10 A5
Weylands BA11 22 C4
Weymouth Rd BA11 3 A3
Weymouth St BA12 18 C3
Whaddon La BA14 11 G2
Wharf Cl SN12 7 C5
Wharf St SN10 26 D3
Whatcombe Rd BA11 22 B4
Whistley Rd SN10 25 A3
White Hart Yd BA14 3 C1

White Horse Bsns Pk
BA14 13 F4
White Horse Cl BA14 13 E2
White Horse Dr BA11 23 F4
White Horse Rd BA15 8 B2
White Horse Way BA13 17 F2
White Row Hill BA14 12 B3
Whitechapel La BA11 3 B1
Whitecroft BA13 16 C6
Whiteheads La BA15 9 F2
Whitehill BA15 9 H2
Whiteland Rise BA13 17 H3
Whitemill La BA11 24 A1
Whiterow Pk BA14 12 B2
Whites Cnr SN12 4 F2
Whitestone Rd BA11 23 F4
Whitewell Pl BA11 3 A6
Whitewell Rd BA11 3 A6
Whitfield Cl BA12 19 G3
Whittox La BA11 3 B4
Whitworth Rd BA11 24 C2
Wick La SN10 26 D6
Wicker Hill BA14 3 B1
Wickfield SN10 26 D6
Wickham Rise BA11 22 D5
Widbrook Hill,
 Bradford-on-Avon BA15 9 H6
Widbrook Hill,
 Trowbridge BA14 10 A3
Widbrook Mdw BA14 10 A6
Widbrook Vw BA15 9 H4
Wilcot Cl BA14 12 D2
William Rd SN10 27 F6
Willoughby Cl BA13 17 E4
Willow Cl SN12 7 B5
Willow Cres BA12 19 E1
Willow Dr SN10 27 G2
Willow Gro,
 Trowbridge BA14 12 C2
Willow Gro,
 Westbury BA13 17 E3
Willow Vale BA11 3 C4
Willow Vw BA14 12 D5
Wilson Sq BA11 19 G2

Wilton Dr BA14 13 E
Wiltshire Cres SN12 7 D
Wiltshire Dr BA14 12 D
Wiltshire Way BA13 17 G
Wiltshires Barton BA11 3 A
Winchester Cl BA14 12 D
Windermere Rd BA14 11 E
Windsor Av SN12 7 B
Windsor Cres BA11 22 D
Windsor Dr,
 Devizes SN10 27 G
Windsor Dr,
 Trowbridge BA14 12 C
Windsor Dr,
 Westbury BA13 17 H
Windsor Rd BA14 13 E
Wine St,
 Bradford-on-Avon BA15 9 E
Wine St, Devizes BA15 26 D
Wine St, Frome BA11 3 A
Wine Street Ter BA15 9 E
Wingfield Rd BA14 3 A
Winscombe Ct BA13 23 F
Winsley Rd BA15 8 C
Winston Rd SN12 7 A
Winterslow Rd BA14 12 C
Withy Cl BA14 11 E
Wivenhoe Ct BA14 23 F
Woburn Cl BA14 10 A
Woodborough Cl BA14 11 E
Woodcock Gdns BA12 19 G
Woodcock Ind Est
BA12 19 G
Woodcock La BA14 19 F
Woodcock Pk BA12 19 G
Woodcock Rd BA12 19 G
Woodcombe SN12 6 E
Woodhayes Rd BA11 23 F
Woodhouse Gdns BA14 11 H
Woodland Ind Est BA13 11 H
Woodland Rd,
 Frome BA11 3 B
Woodland Rd,
 Warminster BA12 18 C
Woodland Vw BA13 16 B
Woodland Way SN10 26 D
Woodlands Edge BA14 11 F
Woodman Mead BA12 5 E
Woodmand BA14 5 E
Woodmill Ter BA14 11 G
Woodrow Rd SN12 6 C2
Woodside Cotts BA14 13 H
Woodstock Gdns SN12 7 C
Woolley Cl BA14 9 G
Woolley Dr BA15 9 G
Woolley Grn BA15 9 H
Woolley St BA15 9 F
Woolley Ter BA15 9 F
Woolpack Mdws BA14 13 E
Worsted Cl BA14 13 F
Wren Cl, Frome BA11 23 F
Wren Cl,
 Warminster BA12 18 C5
Wren Ct BA14 10 B6
Wyatt Cl SN10 25 D1
Wychelm BA11 23 F4
Wyke Rd BA14 11 E1
Wylye Cl BA12 18 D4
Wylye Rd BA12 18 D5
Wynford Rd BA11 23 F4
Wynsome St BA14 12 A5
Wythburn Rd BA11 23 F5
Wyvern Cl SN10 27 H1
Wyvern Walk BA13 17 E2
Wyville Rd BA11 23 F5

Yard Ct BA12 19 F3
Yarn Ter BA14 13 E1
Yeoman Way BA14 12 D1
Yeomans Lodge BA11 24 A1
Yerbury St BA14 3 D1
York Bldgs BA14 10 D4
York BA11 3 A4